"Every one of us is made fo[

thinking about intimacy and sex that goes beyond youth group oversimplifica-
tions? Yes—and in *Knowing and Being Known*, Erin F. Moniz shows the way. She
guides readers past behavior obsession to the cultivation of virtue. She imparts
wisdom, grace, and love in place of shame. She has life-giving medicine and a road
map out of the epidemic of loneliness. Every leader in the church should make this
book a part of their pastoral practice."

Todd Hunter, author of *What Jesus Intended*

"What a breath of fresh air! If you've ever wondered why Christian sexual ethics
seem to be limited to 'stay a virgin until you're married and then have lots of sex
later,' get ready for Erin Moniz to replace this anemic way of thinking with a robust
theology of intimacy. And that theology challenges so much of what we've been
taught: that marriage is the pinnacle; that romance is the point; that sex is the
center of everything. What would happen if our churches focused less on stressing
marriage and more on creating a culture of wholeness, health, and the vulnerability
that is intimacy's currency? Erin's vision of churches transformed by real intimacy
is both scary and exciting—and I'm ready for it!"

Sheila Wray Gregoire, founder of BareMarriage.com and coauthor of *The Great
Sex Rescue*

"At one level, this book may strike you as old hat. Yet another book on relationships
and faith by an evangelical Christian author? But look closer. Here is a sensitive
study of intimacy written by a seasoned pastor, informed by extensive fieldwork,
leavened with wit and humor, and—above all—strikingly in tune with the over-
arching story as well as the micro details of the Bible's grand story of redemption
in Christ. If you or someone you know longs for deeper friendships, and especially
if you work with emerging adults, this book will enlighten, instruct, inspire, and
equip you for the lifelong work of nurturing mutual love."

Wesley Hill, associate professor of New Testament at Western Theological Seminary

"In her book *Knowing and Being Known*, longtime campus pastor Erin Moniz gives
us two sacred gifts: a theology of intimacy borne out of a robust examination of the
Scriptures and a research-based road map for how to form intimate relationships
that are healthy and sustainable. With all the confusion about what intimacy is and
isn't, the church desperately needs a book like *Knowing and Being Known*. May we
use it in both our disciple making and our evangelism!"

Rob Dixon, senior fellow with the InterVarsity Institute and author of *Together in
Ministry: Women and Men in Flourishing Partnerships*

"This wise, timely, and practical book reminds us that real intimacy is far more—and far better—than just sex. Erin's words are a gift to any person, single or married, who longs to cultivate a life of deep relational intimacy. In other words, they are a gift to us all."

Gregory Coles, author of *Single, Gay, Christian* and *No Longer Strangers*

"In an American Christian context awash in pragmatic—but often reductive—takes on marriage implying that marital intimacy is the best or only way to address loneliness, Moniz points us to a robust, theologically rich, and biblical understanding of intimacy. Amid our epidemic of loneliness, she expertly offers us humane, approachable, and expansive theological resources to broaden our imagination about friendship, love, and the relationships that shape our lives. This book shows how the gospel is good news for relationships and points the way toward greater relational flourishing for us all."

Tish Harrison Warren, Anglican priest and author of *Liturgy of the Ordinary* and *Prayer in the Night*

"Young people are longing for connection—in family, in friendship, in romance—but too often, Christian resources on relationships are trite and theologically superficial. Erin Moniz instead offers a rich and robust theological account of intimacy, an account rooted in the triune nature of God, the story of the gospel, and the unshakable reality of our beloved-ness. *Knowing and Being Known* is an honest, insightful, and essential resource for engaging one of the most urgent pastoral issues of our day."

Zachary Wagner, author of *Non-Toxic Masculinity* and director of programs at the Center for Pastor Theologians

"Rev. Erin F. Moniz is a wise and compassionate guide through the precarious landscape of intimate relationships and Christian faith today. Rooted in the gospel and drawing on psychology, sociology, and theology, *Knowing and Being Known* offers a much-needed analysis of how we got here and illumines a faithful path forward."

Emily Hunter McGowin, associate professor of theology at Wheaton College and author of *Households of Faith*

KNOWING AND

*Hope for
All Our Intimate
Relationships*

Erin F.
Moniz

BEING KNOWN

An imprint of InterVarsity Press
Downers Grove, Illinois

InterVarsity Press
P.O. Box 1400 | Downers Grove, IL 60515-1426
ivpress.com | email@ivpress.com

©2025 by Erin Faith Moniz

InterVarsity Press® is the publishing division of InterVarsity Christian Fellowship/USA®. For more information, visit intervarsity.org.

All Scripture quotations, unless otherwise indicated, are taken from The Holy Bible, New International Version®, NIV®. Copyright © 1973, 1978, 1984, 2011 by Biblica, Inc.™ Used by permission of Zondervan. All rights reserved worldwide. www.zondervan.com. The "NIV" and "New International Version" are trademarks registered in the United States Patent and Trademark Office by Biblica, Inc.™

While any stories in this book are true, some names and identifying information may have been changed to protect the privacy of individuals.

The publisher cannot verify the accuracy or functionality of website URLs used in this book beyond the date of publication.

Cover design: Faceout Studio, Spencer Fuller
Interior design: Daniel van Loon
Images: © Fine Art Photographic / Stone via Getty Images

ISBN 978-1-5140-1003-7 (print) | ISBN 978-1-5140-1004-4 (digital)

Printed in the United States of America ♾

Library of Congress Cataloging-in-Publication Data
Names: Moniz, Erin F. author.
Title: Knowing and being known : hope for all our intimate relationships / Erin F. Moniz.
Description: Downers Grove, IL: InterVarsity Press, [2025] | Includes bibliographical references.
Identifiers: LCCN 2024046206 (print) | LCCN 2024046207 (ebook) | ISBN 9781514010037 (paperback) | ISBN 9781514010044 (ebook)
Subjects: LCSH: Intimacy (Psychology)–Religious aspects–Christianity.
Classification: LCC BV4597.53.I55 M66 2025 (print) | LCC BV4597.53.I55 (ebook) | DDC 248.4–dc23/eng/20241208
LC record available at https://lccn.loc.gov/2024046206
LC ebook record available at https://lccn.loc.gov/2024046207

32 31 30 29 28 27 26 25 | 13 12 11 10 9 8 7 6 5 4 3 2 1

To the crowds in my front hallway,

the lovelies in my living room,

the few friends in my kitchen,

and the three brave beloveds who

have occasionally made it to my study.

FOR YOUR LONELINESS AND MINE.

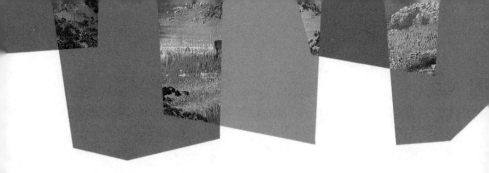

Contents

This Is Not Another Hot Take on Relationships

"I almost didn't come."

We were talking in the parish hall of a church after I had given a presentation on dating and the kingdom of God. Michaela was in her thirties and single. Like me, she had grown up in purity culture and was familiar with many of the influences that shaped me as a White evangelical coming of age in the church. Her admission was rooted in a well-earned skepticism about seminars like mine. She had read the books, seen the video series, and sat through sermon after sermon about Christian dating and marriage.

"It's all the same," she said, "I thought this would be too."

I knew exactly what she meant.

When Michaela and I compared notes, we realized that between us we had close to twenty identical resources starting in the early 1990s to the present that we had both consumed in hopes of finding better answers for questions about intimate relationships. Once I became a college minister, I also picked up any resources my students were consuming. This included books, Instagram/TikTok influencers, and celebrity pastors who were putting out content that has been forming the next generation of Christians.

Much of the informal research for this book comes from a large collection of resources from my and Michaela's era to the present. I refer to this canon of work with a general critique, so I would like to make a few underlying claims about these resources before diving into the analysis.

1. I don't name specific Christian relationship books. With eighty-plus books it would be unfair and impossible to do an exhaustive analysis of them all or to single out certain ones for special critique.

2. I acknowledge that these resources contain good and valuable content that has and can help Christians with their relationships. In fact, I cite several wonderful resources throughout this book. My critique is not a total disparaging of this collection.

3. I have yet to encounter a resource that covers a larger body of intimate relationships that also provides a gospel framework for intimacy. Many of the resources focus on helping with behaviors and choices, but often lack content that produces Christians who are more mature. In discipleship, the approach to subjects of intimacy has been slowly and systematically unmoored from the fundamentals of Christ's gospel and mission. I unpack this analysis in the results of my research project.

There is a relentless sameness that Michaela recognizes about her own journey that I want to highlight here. I felt a similar redundancy in my own experience with Christian resources about intimate relationships, but before I started my research, I could not put my finger on it. With so many resources written and produced, it seems reductionistic to claim that they are all somehow the same.

But from 2017 to 2021, I got my chance to search for answers.

I began a doctoral program that was designed to serve the emerging adults that I minister to daily. My thesis was driven by this problem statement: emerging adults (eighteen to twenty-nine years old respectively) are struggling with their intimate relationships because they lack a robust theology of intimacy. At the start, I had no idea where this "robust theology of intimacy" was found or what it was, but I was given the chance to conduct some peer-reviewed research and, hopefully, glean help for my own ministry to emerging adults.

That project is the basis for this book. Throughout these pages you will hear from the emerging adults who participated in interviews and focus groups. They are male and female, single and married, queer and straight, from a variety of ethnic and cultural backgrounds. To center my analysis on the role of traditional Christian formation in their lives, I selected research participants who considered themselves committed and thriving Christians and could articulate their lived faith to that effect. These participants generously provided thoughtful and candid responses that are showcased here. I offer the results of the ethnographic study as well as my biblical and theological analysis of a theology of intimacy. The questions I used in my research are the building blocks of my critique of the influences of Christendom and secular culture on pervasive ideas held about intimacy.

But my research did not end there. For this book, I pulled from my own upbringing, but I also continued to study these topics as they are being experienced in my current pool of college students. When I meet people like Michaela, I learn more about the unique but also shared experiences and expectations that are addressed in this book. But my drive to write this is not from academic curiosity. There is an urgency to these topics that is fueled by pain points.

For Michaela and so many others, the need for resources about a theology of intimacy is not born of simple theological curiosity. For many of the emerging adults in that room where I gave my talk something urgent and important was at stake. Whether weariness of disappointment, scars from toxic or traumatic relationships, or the grinding ache of loneliness, single, engaged, and married Christians are thirsting for applicable wisdom that will enhance their intimate relationships and keep their despair at bay.

My hope is that my research and analysis will provide a foundation and a reframing for how these subjects are tackled in Christian discipleship. This book is more about the what and why than the how. And I hope that this foundation will be a launching pad for many fresh resources about friendship, family, romance, and all the relevant topics that orbit these relationships.

What to Expect

In the first section of this book, we get a detailed look at the problem. I share what emerging adults told me, and I expose the various forces driving our content creation and ministry strategies. I look at society broadly and then back at Christendom through the lens of my research subjects. This allows us to name the frustrations emerging adults are experiencing and how they are attempting to handle them. While my context is niche, their experiences are not. I take a long look at Christian culture and what we have learned and continue to learn about intimacy from our traditional Christian formation. We also discover the hope found as even our poorly constructed questions are leading us to better questions and to the gospel of Christ.

The second section of the book introduces us to a robust theology of intimacy found in the meta-narrative, or overarching story, of Scripture and not just in proof texts about sexual behavior. We look at the rich truth of the gospel found in the inauguration of the kingdom of God in Christ and what any of it has to do with our intimate relationships (quite a lot, actually!). By recapturing and re-centering the gospel in our approach to intimacy, we can unpack the ways it challenges our secular liturgies. We discover how it postures us to live in both a broken and redemptive economy where we can combat shame and scarcity with moves toward healthy relationships. We do this while receiving and giving grace for all the ways we fall short.

The last section of the book sorts out what we do with these revelations by addressing implications for the local church. I explore how a robust theology of intimacy actually addresses our loneliness, shame, sin, and frustrations. With a look at all our intimate relationships, I offer how the local church can take real steps to be an environment that nurtures healthy, sustainable relationships that lead us directly back to the triune God and our identity in Christ.

This Is for You

Whether married, single, divorced, widowed, celibate, sexually active, this book is for you. Intimacy is a subject relevant to all ages. There is no stage of life where we do not have particularities of intimacy to navigate. If this was just a book about how to date well in an age of apps, or how to raise Christian toddlers, or how to care for your aging parents, then we might need to narrow down the audience. But this book takes a wider look at intimacy and the whole of our Christian lives in relationship with God and each other.

Underneath our questions about side-hugs, purity, abuse, family drama, singleness, and heartbreak I found something more abiding and fundamental to our humanity that informs all of these things. A robust theology of intimacy has more to do with our identity in Christ than simply our behaviors. At the heart of this is an urge to know others and be known intimately. At the heart is the very substance of the gospel of Christ. So you—yes you—belong here. There is something here for you. Whether you are an emerging adult or someone who loves, cares for, and ministers to emerging adults, or a person interested in discovering how the gospel shapes our intimate relationships, you are welcome here.

I want you to have healthy, intimate relationships. Together we can be known and learn how to deeply know God and his love that pours into us and through us from and for others.

Part One

THE PROBLEM WITH INTIMACY

One of the moral diseases we communicate to one another in society comes from huddling together in the pale light of an insufficient answer to a question we are afraid to ask.

THOMAS MERTON, *NO MAN IS AN ISLAND*

Defining Intimate Relationships

Don't be deceived, my dear brothers and sisters. Every good and perfect gift
is from above, coming down from the Father of the heavenly lights, who
does not change like shifting shadows. He chose to give us birth through
the word of truth, that we might be a kind of firstfruits of all he created.

JAMES 1:16-18

Perhaps to really know another person, you have to have a
glimmer of how they experience the world. To really know
someone, you have to know how they know you.

DAVID BROOKS

"I can live without sex, but I cannot live without intimacy."

I was participating in a conference where a fellow college minister was speaking. But this talk was specifically about her commitment to a celibate life. When I heard these words from the stage, it was like someone hit the brakes too hard in my mind. "I can live without sex," I repeated to myself, "but I cannot live without intimacy."

Days, weeks, and even months after hearing this maxim, it swirled in my thoughts, each time bringing along with it the same two questions: "What are we talking about when we use the word *intimacy*? And why would intimacy be necessary?"

The beauty, or annoyance, of questions like these is that they operate much like a Rube Goldberg machine. One question hits the domino, that flips the switch of another question, that launches the pencil into the cup that tips over and releases the toy car, that glides down the chute, and so on. For example, if it is true that intimacy is essential for life, why are we all so lonely? Can we live a full life without sex? Where does intimacy come from?

But if I can risk starting with an honest question I never thought to ask, until I was confronted with finding a theology of intimacy, my favorite one is this: *Should Christians be better than non-Christians at relationships, and why?*

When I asked this in my research, an overwhelming majority of responses from my emerging adults conceded that, yes, there should be something about the Christian faith that produces Christ-followers who are contributing to healthy, sustainable, flourishing relationships. Though many could not articulate what it is specifically about Christian teachings and practices that would make this happen, they agreed that the general premise of Christianity at the very least should orient Christians toward healthy relationships. But wait, there's more.

Despite the initial consensus, there was another consensus: that the best examples of healthy relationships in their lives were from non-Christians. In fact, my respondents lamented that some of the worst examples of relationships they knew of were relationships between so-called Christians. In the end, it was apparent that the lived experience of my emerging adults did not match their ideology about faith and relationships.

But you don't have to take my word for it. Research tracks divorce rates across faith traditions. Even with variables applied for church attendance, regular prayer, and frequency of Scripture reading, the stats between those who profess a Christian faith and those who do not are neck and neck in divorce and separation.[1] Even more disturbing is the research on the prevalence of domestic violence in highly religious households. The #MeToo and #ChurchToo movements bring their own illumination. My students are observing these disparities played out before their eyes.

Yet there is also research that supports how religious adherence and participation actually increases social capital and decreases loneliness.

Faith communities help us deal
and unique support systems.[2]
thread where five atheists we
joining a church just to have
to help with life's struggles

As my emerging adult
leading out as examples   ps, but something
is off. In my search f   . was initially confronted with
a problem about questions.

Are We Asking the Right Questions? Escaping the Quagmire

My students have no shortage of relationship questions that find their way into my pastoral care sessions. I'll bet that you come to these subjects with many questions of your own:

What do I do if no one wants to date me?
Does God care if I have sex with my girlfriend?
Why do my friends always hang out without me?

But over years of ministry, I noticed that I was encountering very similar questions, topics, and frustrations from my students about their relationship woes. Even with new generations coming to my office, something felt redundant, like I was stuck in a revolving door of topics that cycled through each group of emerging adults; I was always looking for fresh, insightful answers to the same questions. This caused me to pause and wonder: *instead of attempting to find better answers, perhaps we can start with better questions.*

I decided to look again at the topics being highlighted and questions being addressed in the resources my students were absorbing. A cursory look at the books they were reading and podcast episodes they were referencing revealed some patterns. Not only did these patterns mirror the discussion topics being brought into my office, but several resources were attempting to tackle the same issues that were the topics du jour when I was a teenager. My first notion was not to analyze what was being

udents gravitating toward similar

stions and answers for them . . .

nth and year in student min-

in a quagmire of perpetual

ips.

mon series or relationship

talks occurring ...   e. This did not happen by accident.

As it turns out, there is a historic precedent shaping our conversations and ideas about relationships. This hosts a pattern so longstanding that it makes sense why Christian content fell into this pattern without really realizing it.

For example, I grew up in evangelicalism at a time when purity culture was extreme, but much of what I learned had roots in a conversation that was much older. You see, purity culture, like many movements of its kind, sprouted in reaction to another movement—the sexual revolution of the 1960s and '70s. But even the sexual revolution did not exist in a vacuum. Historians help us see how the rise of fundamentalism in North American Christianity in the early to mid-twentieth century spurred on the reaction that was the sexual revolution. But when we look at Christian fundamentalism of the early twentieth century, we see it emerging as a strong reaction to the Enlightenment era.

This pattern has a lot we could unpack if I were a historian. But this implicit shaping of ideas happens in both church and society: the questions and topics that influence our current discourse about sex and relationships are deeply shaped by their reaction to prior movements. But if those movements were also shaped as reactions to other reactive movements, it narrows the frame of topics and moves the timeliest conversations to the top of the dialogue. Don't hear me saying that we don't need responses to timely questions that are raised in our lifetime: we do. But if we want to escape the quagmire of sameness in our questions around relationships, we need to dislodge ourselves from this reactionary pattern. It is worth looking at how modern history has shaped our theology of intimacy and attempt to ask questions that our current content has not been asking. We should explore whether our questions and emphases are based on a pursuit of the gospel or shaped by reactions. Asking a better question can make all the difference.

But there is another, greater advantage to seeking different and better questions. This approach has opened a new level of discovery and clarity for my students.

In his book *How to Know a Person*, David Brooks writes about the art of asking good questions: "I've come to think of questioning as a moral practice. When you are asking a good question, you are adopting a posture of humility."[3] For those of us hoping to guide young people through the difficulties of intimate relationships, it is valuable to avoid jumping to answers and provide time to be curious about the questions. For example, I have had countless conversations about dating with my students, and they all want to know how to do it right and succeed—while pleasing God, of course. Instead of jumping into best practices, I begin to dig a bit: *Why do you want to date? What are you hoping for? What is the purpose of intimacy?*

Now before you rush out and begin lobbing these questions at emerging adults, I must advise that this is an organic process. Every person is different and, as Brooks observes, there is an art to asking questions that is part of really seeing and hearing another person. It is a posture of humility that should curb our urges to rush toward advice that is mostly focused on behavior-management. This is not an easy urge to curb since I want my students to make good choices and not dumb choices. But I want more for my students than just good behavior. I want them to know God and be known. I want them to have healthy relationships, but I also want them to become more mature Christians. As it turns out, despite all their consumption of Christian resources and the helpful relationship advice they glean, these habits do not evidence a path toward Christian growth and formation.

But this observation from Lauren Winner helped me reframe my own approach:

> While one task of any community is to enforce its own codes when they are being violated, perhaps the prior task of the community is to make sense of the ethical codes that are being enforced. Here the community is not so much cop as storyteller, telling and re-telling the foundational stories of the community itself, sustaining the stories that make sense of the community's norms.[4]

To get out of our quagmire and enhance our approach to intimate relationships, we need to alter our methods (ask better questions) and our motives (be Storytellers). This does not necessarily mean we need to incorporate more stories into our instruction. This means that we need to be better at telling the Story. Not only are we stuck in a pattern of redundant, reactionary advice, but our attempts at guiding Christian relationships are not producing increasingly mature Christians. Our advice may be good and sound, but it is still often unmoored from the fundamentals of our faith. The modern approach aimed at helping Christian relationships lacks a grounding in the redemptive work of God in Christ through the Holy Spirit.

In our desire to see people behave well in relationships, we have failed to recognize the very foundations of our Christian faith that enable us to be better. As a result, we look more like behavior police than people who are caught up in the Story that tells us who God is, who we are, and why our intimate relationships matter.

So I began asking different questions and learning from what I received. To get the ball rolling, I wanted to know how my students defined intimacy.

It's Not Just About Sex (but Not Not About Sex)

So what is *intimacy*?

Bobbie, a twenty-one-year-old single woman, observed:

> You can know someone and love someone but not necessarily be intimate. I think commitment is the word I'm looking for. There's

a commitment when you're intimate with someone that you both put effort [to make] sure that you're loving each other well . . . you put in energy to continue the relationship and do it well.

Something you should know about Bobbie is that I have never met another person more obsessed with the Kardashians. I know zero things about the Kardashians, but I have sat for hours with Bobbie while she enthusiastically tells me everything I would never want to know about this celebrity family. Her obsession with popular media like the Kardashians, however, hasn't erased her sense that intimacy is more than sex and superficiality.

I believe that many of us, whether we articulate it or not, sense that intimacy is more than just a synonym for sex. In fact, in this discussion of intimate relationships the following conditional statements apply:

- A relationship does not have to be sexual to be intimate.
- A relationship can be sexual and intimate.
- A relationship can be sexual and not intimate.

In other words, sex does not necessitate or exclude the presence of intimacy. In kind, the absence of a sexual relationship does not exclude anyone from intimacy.

This distinction of intimacy and sex is particularly important because of how sex is often elevated and centralized in our culture and faith contexts. This elevation is dangerous because of how human value and identity is ascribed in connection with sex. One of the lies being sold is that the greatest measure of someone's value is their sexual attraction: if someone wants to have sex with you or is attracted to you romantically, you have achieved some kind of threshold of human quality and value.

Underneath the media we consume, the conversations we have, and even the way we preach about relationships, there is an undercurrent that often assumes the importance and centrality of sexual attraction or activity; at the pinnacle of this spectrum is marriage. If someone is attracted to you, wants to have sex with you, and wants to make a long, singular commitment to you—wowzers! We are mere mortals in your shadow. You are really somebody because you are somebody's somebody. If you want to test whether or not a person feels valued by their society or community based on their relationship status, just go chat with some Christians who are on the dating apps.

Because one's value and identity erroneously get equated with sex and attraction, I have observed a deficit of strong categories for how non-sexual relationships weigh in on value or identity. Equally damaging is how sex, attraction, and infatuation seem to be the main measures for value and identity in sexual relationships, particularly in marriages. Other categories of intimacy or togetherness may be considered sweet, but they are often mere accessories to the imperative of a sexual relationship.

But what if there was something powerful and altogether different that spoke to our value and identity that could be ascribed with or without sex? Can Christians possess a faith that *should* orient them toward healthy, sustainable, intimate relationships? Good news—there is an undercurrent of how our Christian faith reorients not only intimacy but one's value and identity.

The Fundamentals of Intimate Relationships

Intimacy, by definition, is a noun or state of being. But I do not want to define intimacy as though it exists in some kind of vacuum. Intimacy is relevant and valuable when it takes place in the context of relationship. In addition, I offer that intimacy is also action. There is a generative energy in what intimacy requires. Fortunately, I am not the first person to suggest that intimacy is a verb and not simply a noun.

Researchers have been studying the substance of relationships for quite some time. Some of the best insights we have on intimate relationships come from the study of human psychology and behavior that has been going on for decades at places like The Gottman Institute (TGI). In addition, there are volumes of peer-reviewed articles, studies, and books on what amounts to healthy intimacy. Like any field of scientific research, these studies have developed their own vocabulary and frameworks. Being the nerd I am, it takes restraint to keep from plunging you all into the academic world of high versus low "minding," "affective bonds," or "social penetration theory" (yikes).[5] So while my social science research colleagues might balk at my attempt to reduce all their years of research to one summarized list, it is invaluable for our purposes to have a lay person's grasp of the fundamentals of healthy, sustainable, intimate relationships.

As a summary, there are three key fundamentals that every kind of intimate relationship needs for health and sustainability:

- Self-giving love
- Attention/curiosity
- Commitment

These three vary in their use and intensity depending on whether this is the start of a relationship or the development of a mature relationship. But to round out their value we should recognize some helpful sub-elements that give context to how these exhibit in a relationship:

- *Self-giving love:* The giving of oneself in a variety of ways.
  - ◦ *Reciprocity:* The back-and-forth commitment of giving and receiving. Includes personal investment and exchange of resources (social, material, personal, etc.).
- *Attention/curiosity:* An orientation toward and a seeking after the other at the outset, and sustained over the course of any relationship.
  - ◦ *Assessment/managing expectations (both together and as individuals):* Continually determining the health/success of the relationship.
- *Commitment:* Choosing to be with the other over and over again.
  - ◦ *Mutuality:* Mutual acceptance of and respect for one another.

These elements are made possible by two other essential components:

- *Communication*
- *Trust-building behaviors*

The following graphics show how these elements work together. These variables are not singular but have a symbiotic relationship. One cannot simply attempt to love or commit to another person; they must maintain these by regular communication and behaviors that build trust. The core enables the fruition of the key elements:

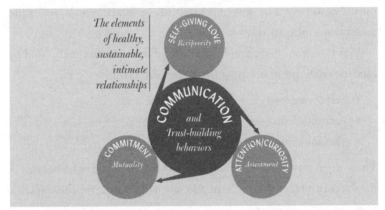

Additionally, the core is shaped by the success of the key elements. For example, a posture of reciprocity and self-giving love will affect and enhance how we communicate and build trust:

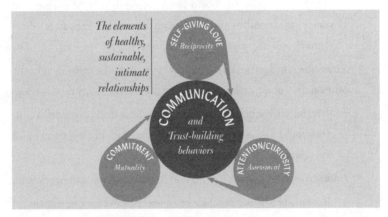

The elements function more like a dance than a flow chart. Each component is like a dance partner working in sync but giving and taking while coordinating their steps. This simplified cyclical relationship demonstrates the postures, actions, and orientations that are required for a healthy, sustainable relationship:

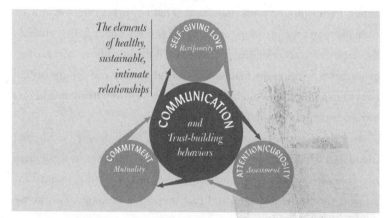

These lay person's terms and groupings provide us with an accessible outline for healthy intimacy that aligns with the research. This graphic will be a guide as we journey through the exploration of knowing and being known.

To use this information well, there are some distinctions to consider between the variables of healthy relationships and true intimacy. First, our lives are full of all kinds of relationships that vary in their level of intimacy. Many of the relationships we navigate everyday are typically not intimate but economic. The gal at my favorite lunch spot knows my name and my regular order. She knows I won't want a drink because I always bring my water bottle. She knows I am a college chaplain and will inquire which book I have brought to read during lunch. It is a nice, familiar exchange that we have developed over time, but I would not call it intimate. Similarly, I can have a healthy relationship with my Uber driver. The nature of this healthy relationship is the understanding that I will pay and tip him, and he will get me to my destination without murdering me. Simple economics. The terms are clear, and we might even have a nice chat along the way.

Relationships with classmates, coworkers, neighbors, and dance moms all teeter on the edge of this threshold between economic and intimate.

But there is a way to isolate and define intimate relationships categorically. Intimate relationships tend to fall into any of these three categories: family, friendship, or romantic/sexual. That coworker might simply be someone you enjoy working with, but if you start dating, this changes the nature of your relationship. Similarly, if the neighbors start hosting game nights, inviting you to their kid's birthday party, and coming over to babysit in a pinch, you might detect some moves from being neighborly toward becoming friends.

As a short aside, I am aware that there is some debate on whether friendship is considered an "intimate" relationship. But in the course of this book, my plan is to convince you beyond doubt that friendships are and should be intimate, and that they are a fundamental way we experience intimacy.

So how do we know if a relationship is shifting from economic to intimate? The key is vulnerability. In fact, *the currency of intimacy is vulnerability*. You don't risk much when you spend an evening with the study group talking celebrity gossip and terrible professors. But once you start sharing something about yourself, something that allows you to be known and seen a little bit, the relationship has the opportunity to change. Not every relationship will become intimate just because you share parts of yourself, but a relationship cannot become intimate without vulnerability. In fact, for every intimate relationship there is an ongoing exchange of vulnerabilities that marks the depth and maturity of it. This is because handling vulnerabilities well is no small feat. This is where the social-science researchers help us out.

The postures, actions, and orientations listed earlier become the mechanisms by which we can develop and sustain deep, intimate relationships. Vulnerability is very risky. I often describe this exchange like giving someone ammunition. Every time we share a part of our self, whether it be information or shared experiences, it is like handing someone a bullet. We have all experienced the heartbreak when someone we trusted with information took those bullets, loaded, and fired them at us. If we follow the tenets of healthy relationships given earlier, we can steward and care for each other's vulnerabilities in a mutual partnership of trust. It starts small.

But this is why our dearest and longest-standing relationships carry the potential for deep wounds. Family is often the most careless about this because we take for granted that these exchanges of vulnerabilities were often not our choice—they just happened because we were part of a family. This is why family, even family we are not necessarily close with, can hurt us the fastest and deepest. But this does not have to be the case.

With the life we have shared over nineteen years of marriage, my husband, Mike, and I have built up nuclear silos worth of ammunition on each other. Our relationship has been so intimate for so long that we have developed the means to destroy each other in ways others could not come close, but this reality does not trouble us in the least. Along the way, learning the art of trust building and taking intimacy seriously has allowed us to limit our target practice on each other. We are still broken people who will be selfish, dismissive, or ill-tempered, but the intimacy of being known and seen and loved by another person, in any relationship, is worth the work to keep our relationship as safe and healthy as possible.

Intimacy requires vulnerability, but to steward those vulnerabilities well, intimacy also requires shaping. Call it sanctification, character building, or just growing up, but along the way we have to change and become better for each other in order to fight back against the darkness within and without that would threaten our relationships. It is in relationships, particularly intimate relationships, where who we are and how we see our worth and the worth of others is developed.

The pursuit and cultivation of intimacy is the journey of any healthy, sustainable interpersonal relationship. From the first introduction all the way to a mature, developing relationship, intimacy begins as a hope that must mature and deepen in this exchange of vulnerabilities. The framework of self-giving love, attention/curiosity, and commitment, supported by communication and trust building, are the postures, actions, and orientations that facilitate a healthy journey of vulnerability so that intimacy can deepen and be sustained. We learn about each other, spend time together, intertwine our lives, and navigate all the obstacles and land mines that threaten this beautiful connection. *The highest aim of intimacy is a generative closeness that refreshes and affirms one's identity and value while simultaneously doing the same for the other person.*

But . . . Jesus?

You might have noticed that this last section hasn't really mentioned God. This is intentional. Remember all those non-Christians who demonstrate healthy relationships? We cannot brush that off as though it were some kind of anomaly. It is important to recognize a common grace in the fundamentals of intimacy. While we recognize that all good gifts are from the Father of heavenly lights (Jas 1:17), we also acknowledge that there are some gifts that are given to all people without distinction. The ability to create healthy relationships is accessible to anyone who would apply the basic principles we have outlined. Self-giving love, attention/curiosity, and commitment are not exclusive to people of faith.

So does faith matter? What advantage is Christianity to our intimate relationships?

When I asked, "Should Christians be better at relationships than non-Christians? Why or why not?" the question exposed a paradox that pushed me deeper into how faith matters (or doesn't) in relationships.

I know all my research participants personally because they all came from some point on the timeline of my college chaplaincy. I know their stories, their spouses, their breakups, their families, and their secrets. I know which ones were wrestling with loneliness, or church trauma, or sexual identity. I ministered to them through their victories and defeats. Some of our relationships started because they came to my office with questions about relationships. Should I date my best friend? Is it possible to be redeemed after cheating on my girlfriend? What do I do if my parents won't follow the boundaries I've set? I lost my roommate and best friend when he found out I was queer—what should I do?

These are important questions, but to care for my participants in the way they needed to be cared for, I began with this other question. Because if faith doesn't really matter then we should just follow the social scientists' research and seek nice, healthy relationships based on these common sense, well-researched principles.

But if faith *does* matter, how does it matter? Jim was a student who came to my office only to tell me that he was in a great relationship with a Christian woman who loved Jesus and it was going well. They were maintaining physical boundaries and partnering together toward a God-honoring relationship. I was beginning to wonder why he had even made an appointment when he said, "So I'm dating a Christian and we are not sleeping together . . . now what?" Growing up in church meant Jim had learned the cardinal rules of Christian relationships: (1) date Christians and (2) don't have sex with them before marriage. But he felt short-changed: Is that it? Is that all his faith amounted to for his relationship?

I'm happy to confirm, brothers and sisters, that your Christian faith does indeed matter in this journey of intimacy. And it is not simply to give guardrails for behavior. In fact, it is about so much more than I ever considered.

Intimacy and the gospel of Christ have an indelible relationship that reframes not only our relationships and our questions, but our very identity. Before I began my research, deep down I believed that there was a powerful undercurrent churning beneath our best practices and moral behavior. Do we want healthy intimate relationships? Absolutely. But what if that is just the beginning? What if our desires, our friendships, our romances, our families, our aches and longings are woven into a cosmic rescue mission to restore our identity and worth against the fear, deceit, sin, and shame that plagues our lives?

So I invite you to bring your questions. They are welcome here. But we will seek to know if there are questions under the questions that point us, like signposts, to the Story that brings clarity and flourishing to our stories.

You can live without sex, but you cannot live without intimacy. This is the story I want to tell you. But this is not the story I was originally told, and perhaps it was not what you were told either. Before we unpack a theology of intimacy, we need to demythologize the narratives and liturgies about intimacy we have adopted from external influences. We must take a hard look at how we got here.

How the Western World Co-opted Our Identities

Their destiny is destruction, their god is their stomach, and their glory is in their shame. Their mind is set on earthly things.

PHILIPPIANS 3:19

By attaching autonomy, perhaps America's most valued virtue, to sexual activity, secular America has marked sexual activity not only as a sign of true adulthood but, more importantly, as the sign of true humanity.

CHRISTINA HITCHCOCK

I grew up loving the outdoors. When I was young we would go camping—my parents taught me everything I needed to know. We would go hiking in beautiful but rugged terrain. I was taught how to read maps and use a compass. My parents showed me that I must always be wary of any artificial magnetic fields that might mess with the orientation of the compass. They showed me how the needle is designed to always find the earth's natural magnetic field and point to magnetic north.

Similarly, as we navigate the landscape of our intimate relationships with our proverbial maps and compasses, we must be aware of the forces at work all around us that attempt to guide and form us. Everyone lives in constant contact with influences from within and without. Everything from our family, ethnicity, geography, technology, education, and media consumption contributes to who we are and how we construct our worldview. These forces often shape us without us even realizing. For our purposes, I'll use two categories that contain a variety of worldview-shaping forces. One category is *traditional Christian formation.* I will define and examine this more thoroughly in chapter three.

The other category captures the influence of non-faith-based, secular variables. Christians exist alongside people, messages, and industries that do not share their faith. Regardless of one's convictions, the saturation of these influences cannot be taken for granted. We still absorb all kinds of ideas from influences outside of our faith. The more we are aware of them, the better we can navigate them and reflect on our own acquiescence. While not an exhaustive list, I point out key narratives and liturgies from outside the faith that contribute to one's worldview of intimate relationships. I refer to this myriad of influences simply as: *the cultural milieu.*

Many of us hold a syncretized philosophy of intimacy that fuses our faith and the culture together. There are some distinct reasons why this is so common. I learned in my research that many emerging adults felt like they were working with an incomplete theology of intimacy. Deeply felt gaps existed in what they had learned about intimacy from their faith contexts. As we dug deeper, it was apparent that there was a direct link between the need to fill these gaps and the infusion of cultural values and ideas. Another observation for why this happens is that it just, well, happens. No one should take for granted the power of these forces. We are all surrounded by cultural influences, and we can be as passive as rocks in a stream to the subtle but significant ways the water is shaping us over time. A third and important reason why this syncretism happens is that even our traditional, Christian formation is formed and informed by cultural influences instead of biblical ones.

Just like a magnetic bracelet that will throw off the calibration of my compass, these forces can lead us astray by creating a false magnetic north.

An Evolution of Values

The Western world is built on values of individualization and personal freedom. Patriotism and national pride often contain these ideals. They are certainly fundamental to the founding of the United States, but harken back to streams of Western philosophy that have been flowing for centuries. Acknowledging that every cultural environment will influence us in ways we may not detect, my main critique is of the larger, general influences produced and broadcast in modern North America. A quick inventory of these values would include *individual agency*, personal and civic *responsibility*, and personal *freedoms* to pursue life, liberty, and happiness.

But these values are not static—they have evolved over time. The off-shoots of individualization, freedom, and responsibility are *autonomy*, *entitlement*, and *productivity*. Why and how these values are exhibited in North American culture is key to knowing how they might be recalibrating our compasses. Each of these offshoots contains significant threats to one's desire for healthy, sustainable, intimate relationships.

In recent times, scholars have noticed that "responsibility for oneself" is singularly focused on a new standard, which is "more psychological than sociological" and points "less to an ability to take responsibility for others . . . than to growing a sense of autonomy" and entitlement.[1] Instead of leveraging our freedom for community wealth and health, the fruits of progress have made us entitled, and this shows up in our approach to relationships.

In the wake of the book and film *Eat, Pray, Love*, there was a debate about whether leaving an unhappy marriage to go on a spiritual journey is self-care or just selfish.[2] Elizabeth Gilbert was certainly not the first to raise this question, but her media content, both personal and fictitious, certainly sparked a debate. So long as I am following my bliss and remaining true to my heart, is it okay if I use this as justification for poor decisions that may hurt people? How far can self-efficacy and self-reliance be stretched, despite how it might negatively affect others?

A sense of entitlement is a cultural value anyone can claim, often without even thinking about it. Mixed with the ideal of autonomy, I can turn my entitlement into reasons for breaking my commitment because I feel entitled to seek my own desires regardless of who it may affect. Alternately, I may break a commitment so I can sequester myself with my significant other or my family because I feel an entitlement to my time and energy. So I will abandon friendships or other connections outside of my boyfriend/girlfriend, spouse, or children. These people become my world in an unhealthy way when I convince myself that their companionship is paramount to my happiness and they are the worthiest recipients of my precious time and effort.

But entitlement does not often act out on its own. The lost value of responsibility is coupled with a rise in autonomy. Freedom is a wonderful thing, but when it morphs into autonomy our unlimited agency becomes central to our lives. It is the kind of force that can falsely recalibrate our compasses. And the signs of this are everywhere.

My parents told me about a wedding they attended recently. The couple had already been cohabitating for some time and neither of them were particularly religious. The friend officiating the ceremony was using a service he found and printed off the internet. It began with the usual "Do you take this man/woman . . . I do," but when he moved to the vows, the couple stopped him in the middle of the ceremony.

"We aren't doing any vows," they said.

The puzzled officiant pivoted, "Oh, you mean you wrote your own vows?"

"No," the couple replied, "We just aren't doing any vows. You can skip to the ring exchange."

Friends, I have been to some crazy weddings. But never have I seen a wedding with no vows! It boggles my mind to think that a couple can rationalize this: "Oh, we definitely want to be married to each other! But just to be clear, we commit to nothing."

The value of autonomy and desire for intimacy pull us in opposite directions. On the one hand, there is a desire for affection and connection.

On the other hand, there is a desire to have connection with the least amount of risk or commitment. The cultural value of autonomy has sold a narrative that reads like this: the less encumbered, less accountable I am, the better I am. It is here that I can be my truest self and secure my happiness. As one scholar observes, "The free individual . . . works to be connected with others only through voluntary contracts that secure his interests in order that truth, love, or duty don't cause him to surrender his own judgment."[3] We eat, pray, love our way to find our least entangled but most true and happy self. We are intent on figuring out how to have both full autonomy *and* intimate relationships in our own lives.

But what about productivity? This value is good, right? I want to make sure we do not confuse the beauty of vocation with the cultural value of productivity. Cultural scholars and thought leaders such as Peter Lawler and Wendell Berry have written at length about the dichotomy of value and human dignity in a transactional system. Under the threat of becoming part of an exploited group, the true measure of success and worth is given to those who can escape victimization by becoming powerful. Those who can achieve this standard of value are often described as "producers" or "exploiters." This identity is juxtaposed against its antithesis: the caregiver, nurturer, or cultivator. The producer/exploiters have value, but the nurturers do not because what they do well cannot be measured or commodified. Their goals are antithetical to each other. One seeks efficiency, profits, and monetization. The other seeks care and health. While I may tell myself that I value the qualities of the nurturer, my consumer culture celebrates efficiency and productivity. It spares no accolades for caring cultivators.

When my godson was born, I remember talking to his mother, Jill, about her future plans. Now that she and her husband had their third child, the next few years would be dedicated to caring for each of these young boys. Jill had already downsized her vocational demands in order to devote her attention to the development and existence of her young sons. Yet despite their best efforts and planning, a single-income household would not cover the needs of their growing family. I watched as my friend struggled to manage relationships, motherhood, work, finances, health, and the evolution of her own hopes and dreams.

Some weeks she lamented feeling pulled in seemingly two directions. On the one hand, her highest priority was ensuring her husband and sons were healthy, cared for, and loved. On the other, she felt the weight of some invisible expectation to achieve and contribute. Even her part-time work became more than just a way to provide supplemental income. "It's as if my value is at stake," she said. "I need to be doing more for my job, my family, and my ambitions all at the same time. I just can't seem to keep up." Jill lamented that her role as a caretaker, while valuable to her, felt undervalued by societal standards. She felt a tug to validate herself as a producer, not just to make ends meet for her family but to justify her worth.

While one can hope that our society is made up of altruistic, caring individuals, the systems of education and industry overwhelmingly affirm that productivity is of higher worth than any other devotion or identity. In his book *Modern and American Dignity*, Peter Lawler writes:

> One big downside of our productive, high-tech, narcissistic society concerns caregiving. Thinking in terms of productivity and caregiving are two very different ways of looking at the world, and at the purposes of human beings. Productivity is measured in money, and that means that its benefits are diminished if shared. It separates us from one another, at least emotionally. It even turns friendship into networking. It's a standard that's tough on people motivated mainly by love. Caregiving is unproductive, can't be measured by money, is all about loving solicitude, and usually seems boring and easy to people obsessed with productivity.[4]

One way this exhibits in struggles with intimacy is in the common practice of transience. I see my graduating seniors struggle with the tension between wanting to stay near relational support systems and moving to where the job market may require. Even after the pandemic opened greater options for remote work, the freshmen workforce is learning that remote jobs are in a steady decline, and they might have to move.[5] Reports from 2023 show that adults are still, on average, moving five to six times between the ages of eighteen and forty-five.[6] This makes intimacy particularly difficult and places a lot of pressure on the nuclear family. There is a romantic quality to the freedom of starting over in a new city or country, but the freedom of transience has both advantages and consequences. One consequence of normalizing transience is loneliness.[7]

We don't often consider our relational needs when choosing a new life in a new location. It is easy to take for granted that somehow we will find friendship and perhaps love. Emerging adults rely on apps. They drive all the way across town to attend a church, buy their groceries, and workout. They hope for amiable coworkers or neighbors. But these are all usually afterthoughts of the main decisions when relocating. For many of my graduating college seniors, they do not even know where to start when discerning the quality of relational connections in a new place. Many are just hoping for a job that will allow for a decent life.

And why would I guide them any differently? During the whole of their education the benchmarks of success are clearly labeled: be productive, acquire wealth, become financially independent, afford comfort. Be self-reliant without being poor and you have officially "made it!" Essentially, when we hail our individualism and personal freedoms, what we mean is that we have successfully detached ourselves from dependence on anyone, and we are now free to be alone. While my students may not consider how transience or the accumulation of wealth and comforts contributes to isolation and disconnection, the narrow tunnel of these priorities can leave little room to develop strong relationships.

Our Identities Are at Stake

People can work at changing their behaviors, but if they absorb the idea that their inherent dignity and worth as a person is measured by autonomy, entitlement, and productivity, their compass will be calibrated to consume and produce. This identity reorders desires. I may desire companionship, sex, friendship, or family. Yet "much of the manipulation of our desires is effected unconsciously. . . . These *include* the desire to dominate, to subjugate, to consume and own, and to control—sexually, racially and in other ways," Sarah Coakley writes.[8] Patterns of dehumanization, exploitation, and commodification of others is more common than it should be. Our very identity is being deformed into producers/exploiters even as we seek meaningful connections and hope for healthy relationships.

Autonomy, entitlement, and productivity are a dangerous cocktail of values. If I can turn persons back into things in my mind, I can reduce others to transactions and assign value to them as I please. I can operate under the myth that I am somehow outside of this transaction of weights and measures, yet that very ideology is absorbed into my own identity.

This is a point I can't stress enough: this critique of culture is not simply to locate bad behaviors, unethical ideals, and distorted narratives. If it were just about correcting bad behaviors, we could learn good from bad and simply choose good. But it is not that simple. The cultural milieu is tethering these values to an image of the fully actualized adult—thriving and worthy, living the good life. It is imperative to realize that cultural narratives and liturgies surrounding topics of intimacy are being tied to our identity, value, and worth.

Commercialization has allowed me to outsource my identity formation, but by doing so my very worth becomes manufacturable. I cannot simply alter my behaviors to escape this. When I believe that what I produce; how well I succeed, and how insulated I can make myself is also *who I am*, then my motivation to comply comes from my strongest source—my identity. I cannot simply ask what it might mean to not rush into a physical relationship when others seem to, because in asking whether I should, I am asking whether I matter. James K. A. Smith was right: we are what we love.[9] But if our loves are distorted by a false identity, how will anyone learn to love and be loved? If our compass is not correctly calibrated, even our well-placed desires to navigate the rocky landscape of a secular society will leave us lost.

How can anyone operate in such a dehumanizing system? Surely I would have noticed this great threat to my relationships and identity. But being successfully unencumbered is often accompanied by disenchantment and disengagement.

Disenchantment, Ambivalence, and Apathy: When Snacks Replace Meals

We are indelibly connected to others. Our lives and our choices will affect others whether we like it or not. This is the nagging problem with entitled autonomy; it is never completely autonomous. I am deeply connected but must find a way to be ambivalent so that I can prioritize self-gratification while maintaining the illusion of self-reliance. This dilemma affects our relationships on several levels, but one of the most poignant examples is found in hookup culture.

B. J. Novak's movie *Vengeance* demonstrates this beautifully. In the opening scene, two young adult New Yorkers have a whole conversation where they congratulate themselves on the art of the hookup. Their justification includes the comparison of nameless women in their phones to searching for airfare; it only makes sense that they should be allowed to review all their options. But this conversation sets the stage for the journey of the main character. The character played by Novak travels from New York to west Texas to attend a funeral of a woman he actually only hooked up with a few times—as the "boyfriend." While navigating this mix-up with her family, he continues to commodify the people around him for his own gain, only to realize that the threads that seem to casually connect them all are much more important than he assumed. In the end, he comes up against his own inability to detach and exploit.

Donna Freitas is a researcher who has studied hookup culture in college-aged students across the country. Having interviewed hundreds of subjects in multiple demographics and across faith traditions, she has published how this dilemma of autonomy and intimacy plays out in the sex lives of young adults. Like Novak's character, Freitas confirms the role of ambivalence and the "skill of uncaring" as the norm for emerging adults to "succeed" at two key secular benchmarks of full adulthood: autonomy and sexual activity. But this produces several unintended consequences. Freitas writes that this pattern treats intimacy "like an afternoon snack for warding off hunger," but lacks the robust nutrition of a meal.[10] It is low commitment but still feeds one's sexual appetite, and it requires the narrative that meals are not that big a deal.

Freitas, who attempts to salvage the priorities of autonomy and entitlement in her conclusions, still concedes that this pattern of sexual activity "teaches young people that to become sexually intimate means to become emotionally empty. . . . They are acculturated to believe that they are *supposed* to regard sex as a casual, no-big-deal type of experience, yet many of them discover that sex is in fact a big deal."[11]

Romance Idolatry: How Sex Became the Gravitational Center of Our Desires

One of my favorite movies is *When Harry Met Sally*. This 1989 Rob Reiner classic has become a cultural icon for the tensions of friendship and romance that still pop up in modern media. But woven in with the humor and witty dialogue is a plot line that distinctly sums up the power of romance idolatry.[12] On the one hand, this could be a movie simply about the beauty of friendship—but friendship can hardly ever hold up a compelling plot line. Just as in this movie, our media is saturated with examples like this: romance plays the leading role while friendship remains a supporting cast. Every friendship in this movie is intentionally wrapped up in a story of romance that takes center stage.

In one clever scene where Harry and Sally have had sex for the first time and are awkwardly regretting it, they phone their two friends who answer on separate lines but from the same bed. This four-way vaudeville-style scene culminates with Harry and Sally both admitting simultaneously from separate calls that they slept together. Despite the despondent tone from Harry and Sally, the initial response from their friends is one of celebration: "That's wonderful!" "We've been praying for it!"

Friendship often plays the comic relief to the leading starlet of romance. Even now as more popular shows are highlighting friendship (i.e., *Ted Lasso* and *The Bear*), the popularity of shows that are made to quench our cravings for romance and sex still reign (*Bridgerton, Game of Thrones*, and *Outlander*). When Disney released *Moana*, viewers witnessed a new Disney princess whose story line was not connected to a romance plot. While this is a significant shift away from the centrality of romance, it only scratches the surface of decades of romantic fairy-tale content. In fact, media's love of love stories can be traced back to early storytelling. The centrality of romance is no accident but is the result of several cultural and social factors that explain the prominence of romantically charged stories over and beyond those that are purely about friendship.[13] In a 2022 study, romance novels topped out as the "biggest category of fiction, generating over $1.44 billion in sales revenue."[14]

We have a romance idolatry problem.

Movies, shows, and music are just some of the cultural artifacts that evidence this with glaring consistency. We have placed our relationship status front and center to our lives by making it another benchmark of true adulthood. But sadly, romance idolatry does not begin with young adulthood or even adolescence. While my friends with kids recoil at the perversion of pedophilia and how it sexualizes children, they don't bat an eye at the insinuation of their elementary-age child having a "boyfriend" in her class. We have an industry of artwork that shows children mimicking romantic gestures. I have even witnessed annual kindergarten "weddings" that the whole class participates in, with little kindergarten brides and grooms chosen by the class. This can be dismissed as innocent, but make no mistake, these cultural messages run deep and start early: romance is important and expected.

Romance idolatry funnels our categories into reductionistic and bifurcated limitations. One can't just explore the nature of their desires, because desire "has become so heavily sexualized in the modern, post-Freudian period as to render its connection with other desires (including the desire for God) obscure and puzzling."[15] There is a strangling out of narratives that elevate platonic, non-carnal desire and affection. In the cultural milieu, romance idolatry is a product of our sex-essentialism. If your worth and value as a fully actualized adult is tied to your sexual success, then it requires that romantic relationships be paramount and sex be essential. Desire is not the problem; but as it turns out, if we define our highest desires as sexual, and place romantic and sexual relationships at the center of the cultural universe, we inevitably end up with disturbing results.

Hypersexualization: Why Can't We Be Friends?

The cultural values that justify consuming as much as I desire, with the least responsibility or entanglements, do not lend themselves to a discrete moderation of behavior. They require a narrative that supports the centrality of sex in romance idolatry. One of the most effective narratives is that humans are sexual animals that *need* sex. This uncontrollable, primal urge must be met for adults, especially men, to fully mature into recognizable adults. The "sex machine" vision of masculinity is a long-perpetuated narrative, one that reduces men to their sexual desire by consistently harping on the uncontrollable pull of lust and the idea that men need regular sexual release to function.[16] To effectively sell this message, males must be objectified and reduced to mere animals with little discernment or self-control. Boys will be boys. But modernity has expanded this message and now women are not exempt from being defined by their sexual desires either. The rise of sexual empowerment in second-wave feminism provides an equitable balance where both men and women are told that sex is an evolutionary drive that must be prioritized and acquired . . . or else.

Mutual objectification is just one problem created by hypersexualization. But along with this comes the inability to ascribe value to non-carnal relationships. Again, this starts early. Jonny and Suzie are friends, but they can't *just* be friends. Whether it's kids singing about "sitting in a tree, K-I-S-S-I-N-G" or the adult version where we badger them about why they aren't dating, hypersexualization limits relational options. Any healthy, platonic relationship must fight against the pressure to be sexualized. Friendship is cast in a supporting role, yet again. It is a mere steppingstone to the prime actualization: landing a sexual partner.

Returning to the phrase "I can live without sex, but I cannot live without intimacy," you can see how controversial the first half of the claim is. Hypersexualization requires that sex is a priority. I need it to be happy. I need it to be seen as an adult. I need it because my innards will burst if I don't partake (or something like that). If I fail to have sex regularly, will I be (gasp!) repressed? There is no way a human life can be meaningful or successful if there is no sex involved, right? Wouldn't such a person be irrevocably messed up? Isn't there some kind of medical repercussion if you live without sex? Surely this prospect is not just odd, but counter to our biology.

These narratives that support our sex-centric romance idolatry have resulted in devastating extremes. In October of 2022, an Ohio man was apprehended attempting to kill as many as three thousand women at a local university. His reasons: they wouldn't have sex with him. This man claimed identification with the incel (or involuntarily celibate) movement.[17] This fast-growing global movement attracts men who "blame women for their lack of sexual and/or romantic success." While this movement has gained attention due to the hateful rhetoric and violence it produces, there are psychological studies and even cultural sympathies for why these men burn with frustration.[18] When we perpetuate the idea that it is our right to have personal freedoms and to pursue our desires, all the while claiming that our sexual desires are the most important and essential parts of our adulthood, how can this not be a result? It is maddening that our attempts to stem the excesses of rape culture and sexual violence are often dismissed in our efforts to protect our right to autonomy and sex. It is very difficult to condemn someone for expecting access to sex without creating guardrails that might curtail our own sexual appetites. If you are wondering where consent falls in this, don't worry, I am getting to it.

In the meantime, Freitas observes that while colleges and universities are seen as harbors of human rights education, when it comes to sexual behavior among college-aged students, they

> learn to treat others as objects existing for the sole purpose of providing them a certain good, to be disposed of or put aside once they are done. Within a dominant culture of hooking up, it is normal—typical even—to use others as if they were without feelings or value. The sheer amount of repression and suppression of emotion required for living in the context of hookup culture teaches young adults (or tries to teach them) not to feel at all.[19]

As a college chaplain, I regularly witness the resounding truth of this observation. The chief end of our entitlement and sex-essentialism is the commodification of ourselves and others.

The adage that "sex sells" is an understatement when cataloging the industrialization of romance idolatry. Without question, we have an entire industry built on consumption. From the promotion of hookup culture in television, music, and movies to the variety of dating apps, we are primed to commodify and consume each other.

Mutual objectification is not a cultural liturgy touted in media. The veneer of romantic storylines obscures how sex-on-demand treats people like functions. But, to make room for sex to be readily accessible, it is necessary that men and women are reduced to body parts. The rise in sexting and sending nude selfies to everyone from strangers to acquaintances to classmates highlights the popular exchange of people as parts for our gratification. If the participants are content with this mutual objectification, everyone can walk away getting what they wanted. In other words, relationships become transactional.

But it's okay because both parties consented to this reduction of self, right?

In sexual or romantic relationships, consent is the first moral rung to hang onto. It is a critically important rung. The problem is that it is also a particularly low rung. Consent is one way to manage expectations to ensure that everyone is exerting their agency and there is no exploitation. Even the culture of consent, however, has resulted in a messy confluence of moral assertions. The problem with consent is that it is not as straightforward as it often seems. I counsel young women on a regular basis who technically consented to sex when actually their yes was coerced, manipulated, or gained through veiled threats.

Now, don't get me wrong; consent is *very* important. *No one, married or unmarried, should endure any actions on their person they do not consent to.* But if consent is the only mechanism for ethical, healthy intimacy, it will not bear up under the weight of this expectation. Mere consent does not make for a healthy or valuable encounter. In fact, the notion that consent is all one needs has caused frustration and confusion for many college students who were led to believe that a willing partner was all that was required for safety and fun. In the end, the social contract of ambivalence and detachment leads to additional pressure and anxiety, not trust building or safety.

Relationships cannot have humanizing or healthy intimacy if they must sacrifice to the gods of autonomy, entitlement, and productivity. Commodification is inevitable, which makes the relationships transactional. Commodifying sex is like any other consumer industry. I could do the work of growing tomatoes from seed, or I could just buy a tomato and have it delivered within the hour. Commodification allows for instant gratification with little personal effort or vulnerability.

The Role of Technology

I would be remiss to make all these claims of the influence of secular cultural liturgies on intimate relationships without acknowledging the role of technology. It would be easy to ascribe blame to the ways technology has changed the landscape of our lives over a few short decades, but it is not quite that simple. Technology is not just an influence that drives values in the cultural milieu. It also holds itself up as a useful illustration of how these values exist and work in our lives.

With the incredible pace of new technology, it is difficult for researchers to keep up with the effects it has on our lives. One common premise is that, since the industrial revolution, technological advances across several industries have made promises to simplify our lives. But, especially in the last century, the delivery on this promise has been mixed. In significant ways, technology has neither simplified nor advanced our quality of life. In many ways, it has moved us backward instead of forward.

In her seminal book *Alone Together*, Sherry Turkle writes: "Modern technology has, all along, caused massive social disruptions to which human beings have adjusted. They have become more powerful, secure, and free even as they experience themselves, in some ways, as more impotent, anxious, and determined by forces beyond their control than ever."[20] The promise of something that makes life or relationships easier hearkens back to the snacks-instead-of-meals dilemma of ambivalent, physical relationships. Jean Twenge notes: "We're malnourished from eating a junk-food diet of instant messages, Facebook posts, email, and phone calls, rather than the healthy food of live, in-person interaction."[21] If staving off hunger is the new goal, then why concern oneself with nutrition? This shift has unearthed a new question that technology is working to address: What is intimacy anymore?

Turkle's thesis in *Alone Together* is that "Technology proposes itself as the architect of our intimacies. These days, it suggests substitutions that put the real on the run."[22] The success of any new technology is to identify a prevalent human problem and present itself as the solution. In a culture that is desperately trying to have both relationships and autonomy, the rise of social technology has stepped in to provide a solution for any insecurities and anxieties of intimate relationships. In other words, it's given us "ways to be in relationships and protect ourselves from them at the same time."[23]

Though not a new phenomenon, parasocial relationships are essentially an artificial or perceived intimacy with someone we do not know personally. This can manifest in our obsession with celebrities. It can simply be a perceived connection to individuals or groups through TikTok, Facebook groups, reality television, or a Netflix docuseries. Regardless of what we choose, there are a variety of ways to enhance our artificial connections to others we have no relationship with. We feel close and connected to people we have never met or exchanged a conversation with. It is another junk-food snack that staves off our hunger for connection but provides no real nourishment or intimacy.

Parasocial relationships place us, the consumer, at the center. They are not only preferred to the creation of new relationships, they are also replacing the intimate relationships that are right in front of us.[24] Many will spend less time on the proximate, embodied people we are in relationship with than we will with the technologically facilitated slot machine of artificial intimacy. "At the extreme, we are so enmeshed in our connections that we neglect each other."[25]

So we continue to diminish each other both in real life and online.

Our parasocial relationships require a commodification of our heroes and celebrities. Dating apps allow us to swipe and ghost and treat each option like a transaction. We can weigh and judge our choices like pieces of fruit at the grocery store. Sexting reduces acquaintances to mere parts. But even these are just shadows and offspring of the most popular form of anti-intimacy that technology can offer.

Pornography

It is no wonder that a cultural recipe that includes autonomy, entitlement, productivity, hypersexuality, and technology would produce anything other than our current pornographic industry. The commodification of sex and bodies is never more clearly demonstrated than in an industry where the sexual pageantry of exploited persons is consumed by individuals seeking the most accessible form of gratification and autonomy. This violence of exploitation and consumption by individuals is the picture of malformation. Compared with seeking intimacy within a healthy, consensual, sustainable relationship, the option to go at it alone at the expense of others seems unthinkable. Yet the volume and velocity of the porn industry is wildly successful and shows no signs of slowing.

But even for those who may not use porn, its effects spread into other veins of the culture. It is changing the perspectives and attitudes of my college students. I've listened to tearful accounts of young women who attempt to meet their partner's sexual expectations that are shaped by their exposure to porn. They struggle with the degrading and difficult expectations but still assume that this is "normal" and what they must do to be a team player in their relationship. One's understanding of desire, gender roles, and how one enters into various types of sexual intimacy is being malformed by pornography. So even for non-porn users, their relationships, sense of self, and ideas about intimacy are being influenced and malformed by the plague of pornography.

Conclusion: Growing like Fires and Not Trees

Society cannot commodify intimacy without destroying its value. Instead of connection and intimacy, people find themselves more isolated and lonely.[26] It is too easy to demote in-person relationships and simply pour ourselves into virtual avenues. Friendship (or other platonic, intimate relationships) gets less attention because romance, particularly sex, reigns supreme as the highest intimacy. And like a sea of salt water to our thirst, relationships mediated by technology, ensured autonomy, and value-stamped commodification does not satisfy. The more we drink, the thirstier we become.

Yet the narrative keeps driving forward. The message of relational gratification with full autonomy is advertised relentlessly in our North American cultural milieu. But the ambivalence and apathy required to support this narrative is having devastating effects. "We have liberated fantasy but killed imagination, and so have sealed ourselves in selfishness and loneliness," observes Wendell Berry.[27] The values of autonomy, entitlement, and productivity lead us away from the essentials of healthy, sustainable intimacy. This is evidenced by the fact that, even with all this technology and sexual freedom, we are lonelier than ever.

"We must learn to grow like a tree, not like fire."[28] Fires consume. Trees develop. Our relationships need discernment, nurturing, and patience. Though no one can fully detach from the implicit and overt messages of the cultural water we all swim in, these forces do not get to own us or define us. Ultimately, it is the gospel of Christ that sets us free and bestows our identity, value, and worth so we no longer feel the need to buy what we are being sold by industries that are not designed for the health and flourishing of our relationships. Like the tree in Psalm 1 that grows strong beside the streams of wisdom, there is hope in Christ for all our intimate relationships. So to recalibrate our compass, we need our faith formation to restore our true identity and provide alternate paths through the rocky cultural landscape.

How Christendom
Baptized Secularization

*I in them and you in me—so that they may be brought to
complete unity. Then the world will know that you sent
me and have loved them even as you have loved me.*

JOHN 17:23

*We realized that giving healthy information is not enough if people are
also consistently consuming bad advice from the wider Christian culture.*

SHELIA GREGOIRE

Charlie Chaplin once entered a Charlie Chaplin look-alike contest.

He came in third.

That story might just be an urban legend but this one is not: in her memoir, Dolly Parton tells the story of when she entered a Dolly Parton look-alike contest—and came in second.[1]

I always thought the Charlie Chaplin story was believable. Even though his face was memorialized in cinema, the media culture was not saturated with celebrity images in the early twentieth century the way it is today. It seems possible that he might not win a look-alike contest, even though he's the real Charlie Chaplin. But when I read the one about Dolly, I had a harder time accepting it. Who could ever possibly mistake the indomitable icon that is Dolly Parton?

But mistaking the genuine article for an imitation is, sadly, not new or infrequent. My students struggle to untangle the values of the cultural milieu and the values of Christendom. My research confirmed what I had been observing for years: the traditional Christian formation of emerging adults was not significantly contributing to their ability to have healthy, sustainable, intimate relationships.[2] But why?

As it turns out, instead of listening to stories of how the gospel was central to what they learned about intimacy, my students told a very different story. And these stories bore out in the frustrations they experienced when attempting to apply their Christian faith to their intimate relationships. I discovered that instead of powerful counter-liturgies to combat the culture's malformation of intimacy, the traditional Christian formation shaping their concepts of intimacy are a cobbled mixture of secular and faith-based ideas about intimacy. The two look too much alike, and my students are struggling to identify which values are from God and which are not.

What Have They Learned?

As a college chaplain, I spend a *lot* of time talking with students about their intimate relationships. While romance, dating, marriage, and sex are the most popular subjects, I admit that I am struck by how often emerging adults also puzzle about other kinds of intimacy. For them, friendships, roommates, community, and family are subjects just as important (and often as urgent) as romance. So when I designed my research, I made sure to order it around these three main intimate relationships: romance, friendship, and family.

I would not regret this choice to widen the scope of intimate relationships. Not only did they have more to say about platonic relationships than I anticipated, but their hopes for both romantic and non-romantic relationships were relatively similar. They also seemed to have a basic grasp of the tenets of healthy, sustainable relationships. But this knowledge *did not* originate from their faith contexts.

They were adept at talking about their faith as a matter of personal significance. They could clearly describe the people, events, and Scriptures that were pivotal to their faith development over their lives. Additionally, when asked to simply describe traits of healthy relationships, their responses came with relative ease. I kept the same order of questions for every interview and noticed this pattern each time:

- Ability to talk about their Christian faith: high
- Ability to articulate aspects of healthy or ideal relationships: good
- Ability to talk about how their Christian faith informs the subject of healthy relationships: . . . meh

Their struggle to connect their faith to their philosophies of healthy relationships required some investigating.

If I were attempting to discover why judges did not pick the real Dolly Parton to win the contest, I would begin with curiosity about any resources they used for determining what Dolly looks like. Perhaps these sources had provided a skewed picture in contrast to the real, live Dolly. Something similar occurred when I asked my students about their own formation.

Where Did They Learn It?

When I use the phrase "traditional Christian formation," it is a way to highlight many possible influences. It is not enough to reduce this to one's experience with their local church, for I would be neglecting the myriad other modes of Christian teaching. For example, in my youth, the church was a major hub of faith development. We heard preaching every Sunday morning and Sunday evening. But we were also at the church on Wednesdays and for special events. Eventually, the youth group became even more formative and important to me than "big church." But coming of age in the dawn of the Christian industrial complex, I was also ramping up my consumption of Christian music, books, and magazines.[3] All these systems shaped my faith *and* my intimate relationships.

While there are influences spanning the generations, my students also have social media, YouTube videos, TikTok, podcasts, popular Christian youth conferences, influencers, and Christian celebrities. Additionally, I included family members, community members, mentors, or any other formative persons in the inquiry. The sum of these influences is captured in what I call "traditional Christian formation."

Alluding to *tradition* does not mean I am singling out a particular orthodoxy or denomination. Instead, I identify something as traditionally Christian when several influences are generally operating out of the same playbook. In other words, when family, church, celebrity pastors, and the like are seeking to educate Christians about relationships, I assume that the central motive is to help people follow and please Christ in how they approach and understand relationships. Even if the ideas vary or contradict, the hope is still to disciple the reader or listener. In other words, if a resource or person's aim is helping young people be "good Christians" in their intimate relationships, they made the list.

I wanted to know where my students were learning about intimacy. What (or who) from their faith contexts was driving this bus of formation? Did Jesus take the wheel?

Someone Took the Wheel. It Just Wasn't Jesus.

Brian, a twenty-two-year-old single male, was navigating a transition with his family of origin. He comes from a strong, connected family that had mixed feelings about any job prospects that would take him out of the state. He was having hard conversations with his parents. He admired them, but knew they were disappointed that he would likely not be able to stay close to home. He lamented that there seemed to be no helpful Christian resources for him:

> I just think it's interesting that there are a lot of relationship books
> and resources, for . . . Christians in romantic relationships. And
> there are so few compared to our relationships with our friends,

and I think that's . . . kind of disheartening. Because there needs to be a lot of growth and we need resources, right? We can go to the Bible as much as we want . . . we can go pray—but I think, hearing people who have allowed God to heal their hearts, their family members' hearts, and people who write about their experience and also help those who are in similar situations. I think that is really crucial that there's not as much for that, for families, healing their hearts and healing that relationship.

Like Brian, other emerging adults are navigating family issues. They have questions and concerns about how to transition from a dependent child to an independent adult with their parents. They are also reflecting, many for the first time, on how their upbringing has affected them. This dovetails into questions about romantic relationships as well as navigating trauma and healthy or unhealthy habits learned from home. Many emerging adults who have left home for the first time and have the space and maturity to reflect on these things need guidance and spiritual resources for this journey. They are frustrated that they have almost none.

Joanne (26) lamented how her formative years in youth groups seemed oversaturated with narratives about dating and sex. It was almost impossible to think about someone of the opposite sex without this lens. She noticed how her own love life in high school and college would have been elevated if she had learned more about friendships with guys. "I do wish that the church—especially in youth ministry culture—that we talked about relationships outside of dating." Emerging adults are realizing that much of what they learned about intimacy from their Christian context is just too narrow to answer their pressing questions.

Who do you follow? Who is right? When I asked about types of content, books were common, but other people were also cited as popular resources. Some of these people they mentioned included counselors, parents, mentors, and friends. You can probably guess that technology played an even bigger role than embodied or analog influences. If taken collectively, virtual resources surpass books *and* people as the dominant locale for relationship advice. Interestingly, as many people cited using the Bible as a resource for navigating romantic relationships as those who regularly get advice from social media influencers. Most cited two or more types of resources they use regularly. They are gobbling up an onslaught of Christian dating advice.

But Stella (20) observed a staggering number of different voices in the mix. She enjoyed talking with her friends about the books they were reading or pastors they followed when it came to dating advice. And while she valued a range of perspectives, she would often feel torn, even paralyzed, by the variation of "rules" and ideas provided for successful dating. Because so many of the resources were based on the experiences of the authors or influencers, the dogma would vary, and it was up to her to decide who was correct. When I asked about her choices, Stella sighed and gestured to her bookshelf and computer:

> Just a myriad of YouTube videos, articles, podcasts, social media types from very theological [resources]. I've realized that I have to look at more than one perspective. And I may really agree with this perspective, but then this perspective really disagrees with this one, but I also agree with this one. And it's trying to put both of them in my head, and I'm like, "How can I agree with both that may disagree?" . . . So I think it's just finding a lot of different sources and being really thankful when they label their theological perspective and call out those that they disagree with because it makes the math in my head easier.

Like many emerging adults, Stella is unable to thoroughly assess where the material has gone awry from a robust theology of intimacy. Another twenty-year-old, Gretchen, articulated the same problem. She observed that Pastor A's book will tell you that you should not kiss until your wedding. Then, Pastor B's book will say that it is okay to kiss before your wedding, but to beware of spiritual intimacy that can lead to physical boundary pushing. Pastor B says it is okay to kiss, but don't pray together too often—it is too vulnerable. But Pastor A doesn't mention the dangers of spiritual intimacy at all. So who is right?

Now take this one example and replicate it for hundreds of nuanced "rules" about Christian dating. The water gets muddy pretty fast and produces a common frustration. It is difficult to know whose advice to follow. What is truly biblical and not just anecdotal? Gretchen ended her interview by saying: "We all have questions . . . that nobody has answers to yet or not that they could just give you. And I think that as a young adult in this phase we have questions about it, and it's hard to find the answers. And so it really is like trial by fire."

Loads of content. Very little color. Though the amount of Christian content about intimacy in romantic/sexual relationships is a proverbial mile wide, this study suggests that it is also an inch deep. While most students articulated a frustration of the often similar, slightly nuanced nature of these resources, my students of color had another critique.

Hudson (25) is a Black male who recently gave up on the popular dating resources his Christian friends were into. He realized that while his White friends did not detect anything, he was growing frustrated with how every book or sermon series was framed in a White context. He saw gaps in his experience as a Black man and the way the resources were delineating "Christian" relationship practices. After looking for Black authors he could identify with, he concluded that Christian publishing and the dominance of White, megachurch Christianity were responsible for reducing the questions and content about intimate relationships to a dominant and niche culture—all the while peddling it as the common Christian experience:

> I will personally get frustrated with [relationship advice from only a White context], because I think they purposely do it. And sometimes if they try to explicitly not do it, it still ends up happening. Do these things work [for everyone]? I think people are just way more diverse than that.

For people of color, the lack of diversity in these resources creates an additional skepticism of what kind of theology they are learning. They have to ask what aspects are truly a part of a timeless Christian ethic and what has been shaped by a White-dominant (or even colonized) culture. The result appears to be an increased isolation, leaving them to figure it out on their own.

What about those fundamental characteristics of healthy, sustainable relationships summarized in chapter one? If Christian resources are using these, it would unify the application even for people of color, right? I learned that few Christian resources regularly identify and apply these fundamentals of healthy relationships. Instead, they seem to be using a different standard and starting point altogether. My students mused that Christians have to think about "a ton of different rules" surrounding healthy relationships as opposed to their non-Christian friends. Pippa, a twenty-one-year-old college senior, found the volume of things to discern and practice so dizzying and difficult that she felt paralyzed by shame and fear. Fear that she was doing it all wrong. Fear that God was disappointed in her. Fear that he would stay disappointed until she "figured it out."

Majoring in the minors: Recurring themes that do not contribute to a robust theology of intimacy. While many could articulate good basics of healthy relationships during our interviews, I was unsure where they learned them from. The evidence did not point to their traditional Christian formation. In fact, their lists of basic, healthy relationship practices and what they learned from faith contexts were very different. Across the board, the dominant subjects raised in their traditional Christian formation can be summed up as purity, modesty, and gender roles.

> I was trained to chant: "2-4-6-8, girls do not initiate!" . . . And that guys and girls can never be friends. —Joanne (26)

Cutting my teeth on the purity culture of the 1980s and '90s, I am well versed in the messages of that movement. I expected that my students, being two generations removed from me, would have different experiences and messages. But the stories they told were eerily familiar. This was true of Pippa.

Pippa recalled a high school event where a guest speaker came in to give the "big chastity talk":

> I remember we left the talk and I got [the speaker's] book. . . . I thought that was my holy grail for relationships. [Chastity, modesty, and purity were] definitely the biggest messages I heard. Do not dress yourself in a way that would disclose too much of what you look like or give off messages of anything that's sexy or attractive, or overly attractive—I don't even know! But definitely modesty in what you're wearing and modesty in your relationships and . . . there's always emphasis on how physically intimate you can be with somebody or can't be with somebody. But then again not enough on emotional boundaries, because those are much less clear lines.

The broken record of purity, modesty, and gender roles contains unnecessary complexity. According to my students, Christian teaching about intimacy tends to overcomplicate relationships. In their observation, it seems to add a myriad of rules about relationships that non-Christians have the luxury of avoiding. I asked them to give me examples of something they learned about intimacy or relationships that was particularly damaging. I received no shortage of answers to this question, but included were laments for things they had *not* been taught. In some ways, what was left out was just as troubling as what was emphasized. Some lamented that they never learned about a healthy sexual ethic from their faith contexts. Several married participants confessed that what they were taught did nothing to prepare them to have a strong marriage or healthy sex life. Like Pippa on the journey to find the godly path to healthy relationships, there was a lot about purity, modesty, and gender roles, but not a lot about mental health, holistic boundary setting, or consent.

And the damage was not only to romantic relationships. They told stories about difficulty in friendships because all they were ever taught was about how to evangelize their friends. Simply building friendships with others, not just evangelizing them, was not a priority. Brian summed up this lament when he noted "[My youth pastors] seemed to care more about rules and scoring religious points than they did about people. They wanted to save souls and [for us to] just behave."

Will the Real Charlie Chaplin Please Stand Up

My students express hope and a desire for their faith to inform their intimate relationships, but the most helpful ideas did not come from their faith contexts. In some cases, what they learned about intimate relationships from these contexts actually harmed them and worked counter to their pursuit of healthy relationships. They concluded that overall, the people and resources that formed their Christian faith were mostly unhelpful in their pursuit of healthy intimate relationships. I wondered about the root of this conclusion.

With everything the secular cultural milieu is selling about intimacy, the church should be the home of God's transforming truth about intimate relationships. This gospel-informed counternarrative should be a robust theology of intimacy that is as different from the secular culture as Dolly Parton is from Charlie Chaplin. But could it be that Christendom's canon of resources and pedagogies on intimacy is not counter to, but actually *compliant* with the secular cultural milieu? And if this is true, how did secular influences get inside our biblical principles? Wouldn't we have seen it coming? We can tell the difference between a theology of intimacy and secularism, right?

One of my favorite bits of historic trivia is about the Great Molasses Flood of 1919. In a northern neighborhood of Boston, Massachusetts, a large tank of molasses burst and ran into the town. Despite the old saying about the movement of molasses, this blobby, sticky flood reportedly killed over twenty people. When I first heard about this, my initial thought was, "Were these twenty people asleep?" If you were awake and saw molasses gurgling down the alley, you might think you have at least five minutes to pack a bag. I pictured something like the movie trailer to the early horror film *The Blob*. Mass hysteria of people screaming and running, and then cut to a brown blob chasing them with the speed and dexterity of an animated sandbag. But then I found out that this "Boston Mollassacre" was the result of thirteen tons of molasses moving upwards of thirty-five miles an hour.

I guess that would be a tad difficult to outrun.

The sad revelations of this chapter are only made worse by the inattention Christendom has paid to the effects of culture on our faith. Maybe we heard that molasses moved slowly, and surely we would see it coming and respond accordingly. But here we are, neck deep in molasses wondering how it got into our living room so fast.

The Picture Is Actually a Mirror: Individualism and Freedom

Myles Werntz writes about the shift churches had to make during the Covid-19 pandemic lockdown. He concludes that the move from inperson church gatherings to purely online streaming was not a hard shift at all, since North American churches were already operating as gatherings of isolated, individual consumers. "One reason that churches were able to glide with relative ease into a season of social distancing and isolation was that, as churches, we had been trained to be isolated for years. What was operationally true in our church practice had been exposed."[4]

Despite the collectivist underpinnings of religious institutions, cultural values of autonomy, entitlement, and productivity remain fixtures in many North American churches. The "privatization of the Christian faith turns out to be little more than a regrettable accommodation to a pagan culture's unbiblical obsession with individual determinism and personal subjective experience," observes Joseph Hellerman.[5] It is understandable after a few centuries of modern Christianity developing in the crucible of democratic, US idealism that these core ideas would seep into our polity, values, and theology. As the New Testament epistles and letters to the churches in Revelation affirm, every church exists in a cultural context that will challenge its fidelity to the gospel with the encroachment of implicit cultural influences. Christianity across the globe must be vigilant to these forces, whether individual or collectivist.

But in our acquiescence, we have allowed the dangers of autonomy, entitlement, and productivity to seep in. Lauren Winner writes, "We have understandably absorbed the story our surrounding culture so forcefully tells us, trading our vision of community for American notions of individuals and free agents."[6] The theology and church culture of North American Christianity is being shaped by secular values, and this syncretism shapes our philosophy of intimacy.

Sex-Essentialism in Christianity

In most Christian resources on intimacy, the overwhelming focus is on carnality and sexuality. Not only have we centralized romance (creating Christian romance idolatry), but we have also baptized the importance of entitlement and autonomy along with it. When creating a vision of human sexuality, "the church is too often trying to oppose with our left hand what we're creating space for with our right hand," observes Daniel J. Brendsel.[7]

For my emerging adults, the narrative that men are sexual animals whose highest achievement of godliness is battling against the uncontrollable pull of lust is the broken record of male discipleship. This is true of Andrew (24) who felt that this message was woven into almost every discipleship opportunity he had as a young man:

> I'm sure some of the things [my discipleship leaders] said were good, but we're at a beach camp. And so the amount of times that [lust] was talked about . . . the scenario is you're walking on a beach and there's a bunch of girls and swimsuits around you. That's just beat into your head in a way that maybe over time isn't as helpful as some people might think. . . . I don't know what the right pivot for a conversation is exactly. But talking about it over and over and over

and over and over again, in a way that likely placed some level of shame on especially women, but also men, boys, and girls of that age.

Researchers like Sheila Gregoire and authors like Zachary Wagner have unpacked the ongoing effects of this narrative and its damage to men, women, and the intimacy they desire to share.[8] Gregoire's research unveils a pervasive but dangerous message about Christian marriage: that men should get married in order to control their sexual addiction. Their wives become the objects of their relief and are reduced to functions of the man's diagnosed uncontrollable sexual appetite. The damage done to these marriages is exposed in Gregoire's data: "You can't defeat porn by simply having a husband transfer his lust and objectification to a 'safe' source—his wife. You defeat porn by rejecting the kingdom of darkness view of sex, that it is only about taking and using someone to meet your needs, and adopting a kingdom of heaven view of sex: that it's about a mutual, passionate knowing and sacrificial serving."[9]

In contrast, there is also suspicion in Christendom of any non-married or celibate persons. Bodie, a seminary student, told me about his work with a local church youth group. For more than five years, he served and loved it. So when the current youth minister left, he put his résumé in for the job. Despite having a great rapport with the youth and stellar reputation at the church, he was not even interviewed. The reason? Bodie was not married. They ended up hiring a married youth minister from a different town, and Bodie still serves in his role as a youth worker. He later learned that his name was removed from the list on the sole basis of his relationship status. He could not understand why being single would disqualify him with such certainty. Surely, the results of a background check, standard vetting, and consideration of his relationship with the church would be sufficient for an interview. He understood the need to be cautious with leaders who are around youth, but these attempts were not even made for him.

What we are witnessing in these situations is an unhealthy power dynamic. It becomes a battle between "the raw physiological power of sexual *libido*, and the repressive power of churches to manage and control it," notes Sarah Coakley in *The New Asceticism*.[10] If Bodie was married, he might have been a top candidate for the ministry position. But the church seems to have few places for non-married people. On the other end of the spectrum, Andrew feels the pressure from his church context to normalize the sexualization of every woman in his line of sight. And so the evidence confirms the verdict. The trend in Christian teaching on intimacy is to condone and affirm sex-essentialism right along with the culture, but with a twist.

While the secular version of sex-essentialism results in an entitlement to sex under almost any consensual circumstance, Christian narratives about sex attempt to place it firmly in the confines of marriage. Romance idolatry does not go away, it just changes clothes. Like the commodification of sex and persons in cultural narratives, the church has the same commodifying system but different currency, and intimacy is still transactional.

But in Christendom, this licentiousness is curbed. It is uncommon for a wholesale affirmation of sexual promiscuity to be advocated for in a Christian context. But since we are not reframing sex in a robust theology of intimacy and we are still quietly cosigning cultural narratives, what we create is a commodification where marriage and virginity become the new currency. Romance idolatry comes to church.

Consumerism and Christian Sex

The commodification of sex and bodies in Christian settings is less glaring because it is woven into a system that is already consumer driven. For years now, scholars have documented the trend of consumeristic religion which seems to have resulted from the basic freedom of religion we have in a country like the United States. This freedom creates a pluralistic religious market and reduces its adherents to common consumers. Despite the stated missions of churches, many are carefully crafted to present a "product" that religious consumers will "buy."

The sticky molasses of consumerism finds its way into every crack, and spreads. Even theology is not untouched, and this makes sense. There is something especially attractive and tidy about commodifying something. Just as technology offered solutions to the tension we experience between autonomy and desire, we gravitate toward solutions that advertise convenience with the illusion of control.

Christianity is unique among other world religions in that it claims dependence on grace over merit. In every other major world religion, there is a discernable doctrine of action, behavior, and orientation that allows someone to change themselves or their existential circumstances. If you aspire to control the behaviors of your adherents in just such a system, you have the tools. But in Christianity, we lack a similar mechanism of control. We do not have the same edge on modifying behaviors through a clear merit system. In our anemic understanding of sanctification in the gospel, we opt to create ways for the easiest and most efficient forms of behavior modification. The consumer-based framework provides us many options.

If marriage and virginity are set up like currency, I can build a narrative that supports a system my congregants will follow. A traditional Christian sexual ethic supports what social scientists have reaffirmed over and over: the ideal for stable, healthy sexual relationships is in a committed, loving marriage. But with so many counternarratives out there, how is the church to compete? Purity culture became the bank that regulated the value of this currency and provided warnings against what would devalue the currency.

While this may have resulted in desired behaviors, the consequences of this system are evident. For starters, we mimic the same approach as culture with mutual objectification. People are reduced to parts, and marriage becomes an environment where our value is based on how we leverage sex to cure the lust and bad behavior of our spouse. Gregoire's findings show that this narrative actually demeans sex instead of elevating it. It reduces spouses to functions: "When there are serious problems in a marriage, telling people to just keep having sex doesn't fix them; it can actually solidify that feeling of being used and disregarded."[11] This is not the story of every Christian marriage, but is sadly much more common than it should be.

Another consequence of this is hypersexualization. Like the culture, Christendom centralizes sex in its own version of romance idolatry. It cosigns the narratives that men and women are sexually charged entities. This becomes the script for how they interact and understand each other and themselves. Andrew's story highlights how much of a burden this was for him as a young man. Every time his church leaders and mentors talked about women, it was almost always in a sexual context. Lust was addressed ad nauseum. He learned to accept that seeing women as sexual objects was not only normal but an understandably constant preoccupation. He noted how strange it seemed that his leaders were simultaneously normalizing the hypersexualization of women and girls, while also telling him he needed to resist it.

Now out of college and married, he wonders about the messaging and mechanisms of what he was taught, none of which prepared him to have a healthy marriage or sex life. He did not receive a robust theology of intimacy. It did not make dating easier—in fact it made it more difficult because the chief message focused solely on virginity. It was as though there were no other tools or rules for his questions about pursuing and discerning a spouse.

And like the culture, the hypersexualization and romance idolatry in Christendom has diminished other forms of intimacy. Friendship is relegated to a supporting cast (if it is mentioned at all). Gretchen relayed the consequences of this in her own experience:

> It was all really weird in high school because I had a lot of really great guy friends, but I felt like I could never actually go deep with them on anything without it being considered something weird. But now that I'm in college, it's been really life giving to be able to

hang out with people, and just get to know them for who they are, and what they have to offer. And share their perspective and learn more about them; not for gain of a possible future relationship, but just because they're awesome.

Gretchen broke out of the hypersexualization that placed anxiety on all her male friendships, an experience she found was actually freeing. By cultivating friendships for friendship's sake, she did not end up on some slippery slope of licentiousness. She found (wait for it) friends. Like Gretchen's experience, others lamented that friendship was not a greater topic of discipleship in their churches and youth groups. The obsession with sex and romance was the same: a person's value and identity are linked to a person's romantic/sexual relationships.

In the cultural milieu, there is a powerful narrative that tethers a person's value to their frequency and "success" with sexual partners and romantic relationships. Christendom does not affirm this promiscuity but has recreated its own version. The currency is not valued by indiscriminate sexual coupling. Instead, maintaining one's virginity—the prime standard for purity—and then getting married become the ways we ascribe value to individuals. Virginity is no longer a component of the larger goals of chastity and wisdom. Virginity, especially for women, is elevated as the gold standard for purity. Why did virginity get promoted over the robust virtue of chastity? Because we cosigned on hypersexuality and commodification. If men and women are sexual animals driven by an uncontrollable pull of lust, it is simpler to regulate their bodies and behaviors than start with a different assumption. Virginity and marriage are the easiest to quantify. But it means that behaviors, and not necessarily virtues, become the rubric by which a successful Christian relationship is measured.

Measuring behaviors in romantic relationships is not the only evidence of romance idolatry. I hear stories every week about the experience of single persons in their churches. Failure to disciple singles or support the construction of friendships and familial support systems in

North American churches is sadly common. I appreciate Joseph Heller-man's observation on this: "It is rather revealing that we feel the need to offer special programs and hire special staff for single adult ministry in our churches. We struggle somehow to fit single adults into a kingdom plan that we have designed primarily for married folks."[12] And Christian singles feel this tension.

Once again, Christendom mimics the cultural milieu. Consumer systems are held up by producers, not nurturers. When we want to assess a person's value, we ask, "What are you achieving?" One's value is tied up in their ability to lock down a suitable marriage partner. Our programming and the way we engage singles in our churches affirms this plan for them. And if they are not marrying, we reduce them to functions. We shift their value in this "temporary" state of singleness to rely on their ability to give their unfettered time to the church. After all, married folks have commitments and possibly children to focus on. Singles are great for volunteer labor, and why not? How else do we assess their value? In a way, we are doing them a favor, and we can pat ourselves on the back for giving them purpose while they wait for their full achievement to come along.

Singles in our churches are in a rough situation. If they follow the traditional sexual ethics of celibacy outside of marriage, their value is diminished outside the church. But if they remain unmarried, their value is diminished, or traded in for a function, inside the church. It gets slightly worse for single females because of the narratives around gender roles.

Elisa is twenty-six, unmarried, and finishing seminary. Her story brings together the threads of intimacy, identity, value, vocation, and gender. During our interview she relayed the lessons she had been un-packing about herself and the messages she had absorbed from her tra-ditional Christian formation:

> I was thinking about those True Love Waits rings—I still have mine
> in a jewelry box. I remember having that ring and signing the little

card. . . . And I feel that doing all those things tied my identity to getting married. That was the end goal for me. As a woman, one of the biggest things was that I had to get married, I had to be a mom, and those roles taught me that being in a marital relationship was kind of the end-all-be-all. It was this message that my life didn't start until I got married. And I really held on to that belief for a long time, that I had to wait for my husband before I could really do anything. I had to wait for a husband before I could do anything in ministry because I couldn't do anything in ministry on my own, so I had to be in some kind of covenant relationship for my life to really start. And to be able to do whatever it is I need to do.

From inside Christendom, our copious amounts of resources have failed to scrutinize how we signal messages about people's value and identity. If churches proclaim that one's identity is gifted by Christ through his death and resurrection, the same institution is in danger of sending mixed messages. My students continued to struggle to find the connections between their deeply held faith in Christ and how they were being discipled in relationships.

Now we can see that our narratives and liturgies of intimacy have little to do with the fundamentals of our faith. Instead, we absorbed cultural values and brushed them with a Christian veneer. We continued a pattern of romance idolatry mixed with entitlement and autonomy. We sustain cultural messages of hypersexualization, objectification, and commodification. Just like any industry, we have embraced the allure of productivity and achievement. So we made our own currency and ascribed value to people accordingly, and we reap similar results of isolation and loneliness.

Isolation and Loneliness in Christendom

Instead of learning who they are as the church under Christ, many congregants attend as consumers and representative households. They arrive and leave as individuals who practice the illusion of community simply by gathering. This is what Stanley Hauerwas calls a "conspiracy of cordiality" in the modern church: "What we call 'church' is too often a gathering of strangers who see the church as yet another 'helping institution' to gratify further their individual desires. . . . You don't get into my life and I will not get into yours."[13] If you want to know whether your church is self-perpetuating isolation instead of connection, just ask the singles, widowed, or divorced among you. Who do they call to drive them home from surgery, step in last minute to babysit their kid, or pick them up if their car breaks down? It is a simple first step to study the "conspiracy of cordiality" that may have crept into your way of worship.

When my students share with me their thoughts about relationships, I can detect the patchwork of ideas they have sewn together. This often includes several uniquely spiritualized practices or ideas that they have plucked from books, friends, and sermons. It might be waiting to kiss until they are married. It may be that oral sex is allowable so long as virginity is maintained. It may be that they think God wants them to be single for a while. I even heard one student provide a detailed plan of singleness and dating rotations he had carefully plotted to curb his porn use. When I ask questions about these "plans" or ideas, my students admit that they hope these methods will please God and that, somehow, some way, they will do so in the right combination of actions or ideas to achieve a loving, committed companion who will secure them from being alone.

In an effort to control behavior through commodification and steer young people toward achieving relational benchmarks, Christendom has neglected any other priorities of healthy relationships. So long as purity, modesty, and proper gender roles are being upheld in their pursuit of the ultimate achievement of marriage to another virgin, the bar has been met.

But what if intimate relationships were not simply about behavior-managed goals but about becoming mature followers of Christ? What if a robust theology of intimacy invites us all to be seen and known despite our relationship status?

Christians, I wouldn't blame anyone for assuming that what we were presenting *really was* a countercultural picture of intimacy. I know I am guilty of this assumption. But despite the running faucet of content, our relationships are still struggling. My students come back year after year with the same questions, no matter how many Instagram pastors they are following. We can't seem to articulate a robust theology of intimacy. And most critically, I have found no evidence that the way we are discipling young people and adults in their relationships is tied to them becoming more mature Christians. We thought we would see the molasses slowly creeping down the hill. Perhaps we thought we would have time to course correct. But in the end, the values of secular culture overwhelmed us and lodged in every crack and crevice of our teachings on intimacy.

The good news is that the gospel of Christ delivers us from this sticky mess with a message of hope.

4

Our Broken Compasses
and the Role of Grace

*But we cannot lay full responsibility at the feet of the surrounding
society for the relational poverty that characterizes much of
the church in America today. We are at fault as well.*

JOSEPH HELLERMAN

But where sin increased, grace increased all the more.

ROMANS 5:20

False magnetic north is everywhere, and its influences are pulling my
students all over the map on their journey toward healthy intimate relationships. If influences from the cultural milieu are not bad enough, now
we know that our traditional Christian formation has adopted narratives
right out of the culture. Romance idolatry and sex-essentialism reign supreme. The mix of autonomy, entitlement, productivity, and technology
serves up systems of commodification, exploitation, and value statements
that breed comparison, competition, frustration, and loneliness.

So let's give out some progress reports. How do the cultural milieu
and traditional Christian formation measure against the fundamentals
of healthy intimate relationships? As a refresher, here is the summary of
the postures, actions, and orientations one needs for good relationships:

- *Self-giving love*: The giving of oneself in a number of ways.
  - *Reciprocity*: The back-and-forth commitment of giving and receiving. Includes personal investment and exchange of resources (social, material, personal, etc.).
- *Attention/curiosity*: An orientation toward and a seeking after the other at the outset and sustained over the course of any relationship.
  - *Assessment/managing expectations (both together and as individuals)*: Continually determining the health and success of the relationship.
- *Commitment*: Choosing to be with the other over and over again.
  - *Mutuality*: Mutual acceptance of and respect for one another.

These elements are informed and held together by two factors:

- *Communication*
- *Trust-building behaviors*

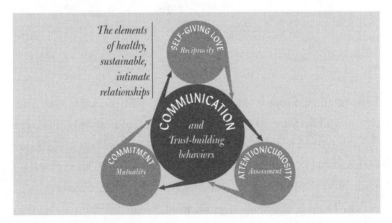

The Cultural Milieu: Free Love, Not as Free as Advertised

We can hold up the cultural milieu, which values autonomy, entitlement, and productivity, against the fundamentals of healthy intimacy and see the mismatch from miles away. In a culture with these values, any relationship seeking intimacy has its work cut out for it.

First, it is nearly impossible to value self-giving love and commitment when we seek to protect our unentangled status that asks as little of us as possible. As Chesterton said, "Thus in love the free-lovers say: 'Let us have the splendour of offering ourselves without the peril of committing ourselves.'"[1] Autonomy is challenged by the call to give of oneself, to risk something, to care for another. In our friendships, families, and romantic relationships, there is a pull to seek individual gratification and personal comfort first before considering how it affects others or our relationship to them.

Second, since reciprocity thrives under the standard of self-giving love, this give-and-take in relationships becomes difficult while prioritizing personal entitlement. In line with a commodification of intimacy, the art of reciprocity can easily be reduced to scorekeeping. Fairness and equity are important to any relationship, but for intimate relationships, the equity of reciprocity is essential. So how might two persons gauge reciprocity in an intimate relationship? There is a need for mutual attention, mindfulness, and caretaking in an intentional but organic exchange. This exchange has no perfect measures for equity and is, instead, a posture that allows people to feel seen and known, which fills them up for a reciprocal pouring out and into the other. This is interrupted, however, when a person prioritizes their own needs and agenda ahead of the relationship.[2] When entitlement is a protected value, the need to assess if my partner is meeting all my wants and needs requires me to shift from reciprocity to a kind of relational scorecard. Yet without another framework, the give-and-take of relationships devolves to pettiness.

Third, mutuality and attention are strained because it might mean conceding power and dislodging our autonomous selves from the center. One reward for ambivalence is that "in any relationship, the person who is least invested holds the power."[3] We feel this tension and have difficulty navigating it. Fortunately, technology provides conduits to effortlessly wield this power struggle. We can ghost, paperclip, or delay our responses. We can be glib or evasive. All of these are not only common concerns in the modern world of dating, friendship, and family, but we have little recourse against them. Many opt in because, if you can't beat 'em, join 'em. At least now I can protect myself with my own ambivalence. And if I have permission to treat people as commodities, my cognitive dissonance is put at ease.

Fourth, in any relationship, but especially ones with vulnerability, consent has become the singular standard. Now, my brothers and sisters, do not take this critique as an attack on the role of consent: I want to be clear again that consent is a necessary and valuable practice of any and every relationship. No healthy relationship can exist where coercion, abuse, gaslighting, or force is used against or to manipulate a person's will. But in a society where full autonomy and entitlement are key, it is difficult to put guardrails on any kind of behavior where self-gratification is at stake. Ultimately, consent is the best we can do to draw a moral line somewhere in our pursuit of a right to sex—and while consent is important, it is a very low bar.

My critique is not against consent, but how it stands alone as the seemingly unanimous ethic for healthy mutuality. I have witnessed consent used as the singular value for everything from polyamory to intimate partner violence. But in the vulnerable exchange of relational currency, merely gaining consent is not the same as respect. This basic acknowledgment of another person's right to consent does not ascribe value or dignity in any substantial way. It is the first step of a tall staircase to achieve care and attention of another. Two consenting adults can still diminish and harm each other because consent alone does not provide all that is needed to keep a relationship (or even a hookup) from toxic consequences.

Our obsession with autonomy is a strong gravitational force that pulls our wills to acquiesce to all forms of self-expression and gratification. If they are consenting adults, then okay, you do you. Follow your bliss. Consequently, we are loath to name anything as "wrong" in relationships, especially sexual ones. We don't want to cramp people's style or be labeled as prudish or closed-minded. That would be (cue eye roll) *so uncool* of us to impose standards on someone else.

The verdict? If the values of autonomy, entitlement, and productivity are protected and prioritized they will be in competition with the components for healthy intimate relationships and, in some cases, diminish or cancel attempts at knowing and being known.

Christendom: I Don't See Consent on the Agenda

But are we any better off with our Christian values and ethics? How does the traditional Christian formation measure up against the foundational elements of intimate relationships? The research is mixed for a generation that was taught purity and modesty as top priorities in romantic relationships. On the one hand, many adherents did wait until marriage, or at least longer than they would have, before having sex. They also had fewer sexual partners. On the other hand, "participants in abstinence programs were less likely to use condoms and thus more likely to acquire sexually transmitted diseases such as chlamydia or HIV infection."[4] On the *third* hand, purity before marriage did not inevitably result in healthy marriages with healthy sex lives.[5]

I wonder if anyone was surprised when purity was not listed as one of the core values of healthy, sustainable relationships diagrammed earlier. An argument can be made that sexual purity is a kind of fidelity that builds trust toward longstanding commitment. I don't deny that this is one possible outcome for couples; it certainly was in my own marriage. There is a foundation of self-giving and care when we can demonstrate a fortitude that shows that we were not simply and only about our own personal gratification.

But this is not the only story, and indeed virginity (or however purity is measured) does not necessitate fortitude or altruism any more than sexual activity outside of marriage can be chalked up to selfishness or low morals. For example, my friend Terry has social anxiety and a disability that make closeness in any relationship difficult. His virginity has nothing to do with purity culture. On the flip side, I know so many students who lost their virginity because they were raped. Purity is a narrow currency that tells an incomplete story while measuring people's value based on a thin margin of specific behaviors.

Additionally, purity is a topic that targets a specific age group during a narrow stage of development. In other words, the ethics of purity have been leveraged by Christendom in large part to stem the tide of teen pregnancy and sexual deviance. But how does purity apply broadly to the overall health of intimate relationships of all kinds and in all phases of life? It doesn't.

It is unfortunate that the topics we discuss most in Christian resources about intimacy have to do with the time between when you hit puberty and get married. My students feel this deficit. It is not just what is being said but what is being left out that matters. What about friendship? What about how we discern who to marry? What about life after divorce or the death of a spouse? What about lifelong singleness, or family? Our traditional treatment of purity covers a slim portion of Christian life and relationships. Yet we have overwhelmingly dedicated our resources and narrative to this. One of the major deficits of Christendom is not that we are failing at the variables of our healthy relationships diagram, but that we have barely touched on many of them at all.

Like values of the cultural milieu being in competition with values of healthy relationships, Christendom's debate about gender roles opens the door for diminished mutuality and reciprocity in intimate relationships between men and women. Popular books on Christian marriage ascribe to complementarian gender roles that establish a hierarchy of men over women.[6] While I'll leave the debate on egalitarianism versus complementarianism to other books, the role of power dynamics in intimate relationships is important.

The studies that hail mutuality and reciprocity as fundamental to healthy, sustainable relationships find that equitable power in partnerships is key.[7] Yet anything that would challenge the hierarchical order of a husband over a wife (or simply men over women) is deemed a threat by those who feel that these gender roles are essential for godly relationships. But a relationship cannot have mutuality or reciprocity if respect and acceptance are coerced or required by a binary status. The essential give-and-take of any relationship is stymied when agency is replaced by obligation. A subordinate can still participate in an intimate relationship, but their motivations and status come into question. Power does not necessitate love or respect, but it does make it more difficult to offer them freely.

Most tragic is when male hierarchy and female subordination threatens the basics of consent in sexual activity. I can't say this enough: consent is essential, albeit a very low bar, in any relationship. Nevertheless, it is a heartbreaking reality for some Christian relationships between men and women, even (and especially) in marriage where a power imbalance finds its way into the bedroom. The priority of consent, which gives equal power to both partners, is weakened. We try to smooth this over by saying that the husband should be kind, loving, and considerate of his wife. But none of these replaces her need to be able to consent willingly and not because she "ought to" due to her subordinate status.

This is not an inevitability in complementarian relationships and there are many couples I know who practice headship but do not extend a power imbalance into the bedroom. But there are casualties of our internal wars about gender roles. Some have fought hard to prioritize the importance of male headship and thus a power structure where women lose the freedom to consent. Partnership is diluted by the need to protect this power structure. In our compulsion to rally support for this sanctioned gender dynamic, violence and abuse have seeped in. Those who claim Christ should ask ourselves, *Am I hesitant to damage the power allotments in gender roles to such an extreme that I would justify violence and other abuses?* Sadly this is still a relevant and required critique.

The verdict? Stacked up against the variables of healthy intimacy, neither the cultural milieu nor traditional Christian formation is helping our compasses work well as we navigate the terrain of relationships in our desire to know and be known. With so many forces pulling away from the basics of healthy intimate relationships, how can we trust where the needle is pointing?

But blame for all our relational woes does not solely land on these factors. There is one more curtain to pull back.

The syncretism of secular culture and Christianity is a major problem, but it is not the only problem. If all we needed to do was change how we talked about sex, friendship, family, and marriage, we could delve right into this de-syncretization. But we don't just have a problem with intimacy. There is also a problem with our gospel.

Just Do You, Boo: Better to be Unhelpful than Judgmental

I saw this gospel problem in my focus groups.

If you want to get different answers, ask different questions. Interviews with emerging adults yielded fantastic insights, but I wanted to turn the tables and ask them to peer in as outsiders.

Instead of asking the same questions I did in the interviews, my focus groups were given three fictitious scenarios along with questions to prompt responses. I wondered what would happen if emerging adults became the scientists. Would they see themselves in the scenarios? Would they detach and judge? Would they be able to articulate a theology of intimacy?

I'm a nerd, so I love a good focus group. And I'm not talking about a sanitized room where you sample snacks and a person records your responses on a clipboard. I left these groups alone in a room with an audio recorder, a binder, and instructions to not come out until everyone had said their truth. No rules, no Jesus points for Christian-y answers, no experts—just raw assessments. I designed the scenarios to push against their own ideas about intimacy, relationships, and Christian ethics. I hoped they would have a lot to say, and they did not disappoint.

Big takeaway: in nearly 100 percent of the discussions, when prompted to apply Christianity to "help" the fictitious characters, they struggled and failed to provide a Christian narrative, helpful Scriptures, or even just ideas that they could confidently tie back to their faith.

Many were quick to respond, "Well, I know how my youth minister/church back home would have responded." This was followed by tropes from purity culture or examples of how Scriptures and dogmas were often weaponized. The groups more readily identified harmful Christian narratives than helpful ones. If they did land on positive or helpful advice, it was not anything that they could connect to their faith. Any advice they could articulate came from somewhere outside of their traditional Christian formation.

Most surprising to me was the fact that they were reluctant to make any moral assertions of any kind. The scenarios intentionally included some ethical gray areas. I wanted the discussions to promote thoughtful and creative ways to approach everything from roommate conflicts to semi-deviant romantic relationships. But in one scenario, I outlined an obviously abusive relationship. I wanted to see if the group would be able to unanimously name this kind of relationship as dangerous. While wishy-washy in other areas, I assumed they would easily support a unanimous claim that this relationship was deeply toxic.

But I was wrong. It never occurred to me that a generation brought up on education about consent, intimate partner violence, and the #MeToo movement would be hesitant to call out an abusive relationship. Yet they nimbly skirted around making moral judgments of any kind. At first, I didn't know what to make of this. But the forces driving these responses eventually became clearer in the debrief.

As a final attempt at information, the group was asked to provide insights to a fictitious local church that was preparing a series on relationships for college students. I asked them to think back to all the different characters from the scenarios. If each of those characters attended the relationship series provided by this church, would it help? I asked them to offer their insights as though they were consulting with this church on the series. What should the church leadership include or exclude from the series to make it optimal for these characters to move toward healthy intimate relationships?

These were their conclusions.

First, there was a consensus that faith-based teaching often felt too rigid or presented as a one-size-fits-all model for relationships. Second, they lamented that the characters in the scenario would not be helped if they attended this fictional church and received the same teaching many of them had received. In their diagnosis, they finally moved toward a unanimous rationale. What were the primary flaws of these teachings? Essentially, they lacked any hint of grace.

There was a consensus that shame and guilt are the driving force behind teachings about Christian relationships. They sensed that the whole point of the teachings was to produce relationships that aligned with Christian values but *did not* necessitate a result of healthy relationships. There appeared to be no place for mistakes or brokenness. One student noted that the local church's approach to college students and relationships should "yes, be scriptural, but also . . . making sure that [they're] not shaming people in any of these situations, and [they're] not calling people out or making them feel like they need to hide, because I think that that's a really hard thing for churches to do well when dealing with delicate situations."

Now I could begin to see why phrases like "don't be judgmental," and "don't push your opinions," came up frequently in the discussions as they tiptoed around vague answers. It was as though the worst sin they could commit was to make a moral statement or impose their perspective in any way. To do so was considered judgmental, shaming, and ineffective. I was surprised at the lengths they would go to avoid truth statements of any kind, even in the face of obvious violations. But as I went back over the transcripts, I began to see it. More and more, I detected an under-current as though all the tiptoeing and reluctance contained a message of its own. These groups ached for grace, reconciliation, and understanding. The overcorrection was an attempt to show Christian hospitality to their fictitious peers. Even though their attempts were no more helpful than rigid legalism, what drove their responses places a spotlight on our own interpretation of the gospel. Do we understand grace?

We May Have Lost the Plot

I can't understate the importance of this pattern. Our younger genera-tions are sacrificing ethics to err on the side of grace. They choose to be unhelpfully vague to avoid seeming judgmental. There is no doubt that secular influences weigh in on this pattern. Moral judgments about another person's sexual activity, identity, or orientation are a cultural anathema. You could get canceled for that kind of thing.

But Jesus is no stranger to the balance of morals and grace. He does not retreat from calling out sin, nor does he withhold a promiscuous generosity of grace. My students all claim to be Christians. They all claim to follow Jesus. Yet this balance eludes them. And, if we are honest, let's include ourselves in this. It eludes us too. We have a gospel problem.

Following Christ requires a seriousness about sin *and* grace. Similarly, healthy intimacy requires guardrails *and* the space to make mistakes. We will never do this perfectly. But how can we discern the balance of sin and grace in our relationships? We need the truth of Christ's gospel.

Lauren Winner makes a helpful observation about sexual ethics and the way we approach them in the church:

> To be sure, Scripture has plenty to teach us about how rightly to order our sexual lives, but, as the church, we need to ask whether the starting point for a scriptural witness on sex is the isolated quotation of "thou shalt not," or whether a scriptural ethic of sex

begins instead with the totality of the Bible, the narrative of God's redeeming love and humanity's attempt to reflect that through our institutions and practices.[8]

In other words, do we ask ourselves what the gospel has to do with these ethics and behaviors we are so eager to see embraced? Scripture does have explicit references to different kinds of intimate relationships and the behaviors therein. But is this all that Scripture and the tradition of our Christian faith has to offer on this subject?

In our attempts to apply Scripture and our faith to relationships, we have narrowed and reduced our body of knowledge. I have shown how the questions and answers we prioritize have been affected by reactionary forces throughout history. This has narrowed what we pay attention to in relationships and has almost certainly contributed to our elevation of purity, modesty, and gender roles. But we have also lost our way in our attempts to use broken tools of the culture to effect change and behavior modification. Christendom has acquiesced to the tidy and user-friendly mechanisms that require us to reduce sex and bodies to commodities we can attempt to control or justify. In our commodification, we have diminished people, their dignity, value, and identity. No wonder my students are so wary and suspicious of applying their Christian faith in the lives of others, even fictitiously. There is something un-Christian about it that they could not quite put their finger on. They could not quite articulate the gospel or why it mattered.

If our current attempts at a theology of intimacy are not necessarily promoting healthy relationships, producing safe and fulfilling intimacy, or contributing solidly to one's discipleship as a follower of Christ, is it safe to say we have unmoored ourselves from the gospel?

Hope in the Mess: Overcoming a Broken Compass

At the end of one of the focus groups, one participant, Connie, made this closing statement:

I think it relates back to what we were just talking about, like the purposes of intimacy are to imitate what Christlike love looks like even though we won't do that perfectly. . . . But I think as a church striving for that, you're doing it because you want to show God to the world and show God in you to the people around you.

I almost couldn't believe it when she said it. After an entire session of obfuscation, watered-down answers, and indictments of Christian teachings on relationships, did this young woman just articulate gospel truths?

Christian emerging adults want to please God in their relationships, and they are seeking wisdom and insights into how they accomplish this. They want to participate in their local church and be an active part of shaping the culture for all people, regardless of relationship status. They are hungry for a deeper application of God's grace and the gospel in how they live in the world.

But it cannot just be about behavior modification, even if those behaviors can be tethered to biblical truths about obedience to God. This is because the heart of the gospel of Christ is not first and foremost about behaviors. The gospel is about identity.

If all we needed was better advice, we could take our diagram, teach people the fundamentals of healthy relationships, and train them on how to practice those fundamentals. But this is not enough. All the scientific documentation in the world hasn't fixed our messy relationships. That is because something deeper is at work. This whole discussion of intimacy is bound up in our identity.

There is a significant question under all the other relationship questions. We aren't just asking how to have healthy relationships. We are looking all our relationships in the face—our love life, our family, our friendship—and we are asking, "What does this relationship say about me? My worth? My identity?"

"Am I unlovable?"

"Am I destined to be alone?"

"Will I ever be able to find someone better?"

"What is it about me that makes all my friends ghost me?"

Our identity, our value, our worth is at stake. Whether we are getting our information from inside or outside our faith contexts, all the narratives are attempting to ascribe identity and value through intimacy, statuses, and behaviors. It is gutting. We feel it at our core. These are not just choices; these are determinations of our humanity.

This is why we need to recapture the gospel and re-center it into our theology of intimacy. Only the gospel can provide the answers we need for this ache of insecurity in our value and identity.

This is true north.

Navigating the landscape of relationships might seem impossible. With so many different influences mimicking magnetic north, how can we begin to trust our compass? It can be daunting to sit with the mess of chapters two and three and wonder: How can we ever find our way with all these other forces misdirecting us? The answer is true north.

Orienteers have long taught that if you cannot orient to magnetic north for whatever reason, you can find true north using the stars or the sun. Unlike magnetic north, these guides are unshakable. They are not fickle and cannot be faked. In our search for intimacy, the best way to unravel the mess and cut through the din of false hope is to find our true north in this journey: the gospel of Christ.

My students have a sense that they are on this journey with broken compasses. Without the ability to fix the culture or Christendom, they instead attempt to construct a different compass or make guesses with the one they have. Using the only tools they believe are available to them, they mesh secular and Christian values in an attempt to know and be known. But they sense that their tools are incomplete. And then, in a rare lucid moment, Connie nails it. So now I have to ask, how do we imitate Christ and show God to the world?

The gospel is still at work despite our failings. We must be honest about how we have gotten it wrong, but we will not succumb to gracelessness. This dark diagnosis of these past few chapters is what drove me to seek out a robust theology of intimacy.

And what I found has changed my life and ministry forever.

Part Two

THE GOSPEL
OF INTIMACY

The problem with relationships is that they all take place right smack-dab in the middle of something, and that something is the story of redemption, God's plan to turn everything in our lives into instruments of Christlike change and growth.

TIMOTHY LANE AND PAUL TRIPP, *RELATIONSHIPS: A MESS WORTH MAKING*

5

Discovering the Origins of
Intimacy and Our Desires

Human existence is a history of relationship, interaction, communion, and communication whereby we become more than what we were. In right relationship with God, humanity is becoming truly personal, truly human.

DANIEL L. MIGLIORE

Then God said, "Let us make mankind in our image, in our likeness."

GENESIS 1:26

"Are you called to singleness or are you called to marriage?"

Is this type of question familiar to you? I know that I hear it asked in many popular Christian presentations, ministries, and books. But I have always wondered about the way we use the word *called* in questions like this, specifically as it functions in the timeline of someone's story. For example, what about my friend Jane who didn't get married until she was forty? Was she called to singleness for much of her young adulthood and then received a different call to marriage? What about my former students Tanya and Chip who got married right out of college and divorced three years later? Are they called to marriage or to singleness? What about my colleague Mark? He married Maria in their thirties after a few years of dating. But a fatal disease took her a week after their first wedding anniversary. Is he now called to singleness?

If I'm being honest, a great deal of frustration over intimate relationships is bound up in a simple question: *How much of this is God (or fate) and how much of it is on me?* It seems that everyone struggles with a kind of cryptic puzzle over the role of the metaphysical. And you don't have to be a Christian to struggle with this. Fate is a rampant theme in romantic comedies; movies like *Only You* or *Serendipity* star a leading lady frazzled over the role of fate in her love life to the point of disillusionment.

While attempting to navigate the difficulty of romance, dating, marriage, and sex, we are burdened by the additional complications of having to decode the message being sent to us by God or the universe. This unseen force, whether named as God or fate, is a phantom variable. It is a man behind the curtain pulling levers while we fixate on the light show, feeling helpless. No wonder astrological signs have become popular again. Prayer not working? Ask the ancient wisdom of the stars. Whether it's the role of fate, or astrology, or God, we hope that something or someone is pulling cosmic levers on our behalf. We seek comfort in this possibility because the burden of our own loneliness and desires can be daunting.

Can we get real for a sec? I am thinking about a friend I heard from just moments ago. Today happens to be both Ash Wednesday and Valentine's Day. Leslie is single, and this was already going to be a hard week for her because her little sister is getting married this weekend. But today was pure grief. Stuff happened at work, she had car trouble, and even with the cloak of Ash Wednesday to pave the road for lament, the stab of Valentine's Day and the impending wedding was just gutting. She cried for the millionth time today as she told me, "It just feels so unfair!"

You may identify.

It made me think of another friend, Ali, who has two kids. They went to dinner at a friend's house, and she told me how being with another family in their home was a challenge. One of her children has special needs, but being with the other family and their kids illuminated a stark contrast. It exposed her chaotic life against a household more subdued.

This was not only embarrassing, but shameful. And she wondered, *Why do we have these kids and this lot?* Ali and her husband pour so much energy into their kids and it is exhausting. She loves her children, but confessed, "These were not the kids I thought I would have."

Who is responsible for these variables I can't seem to control? Leslie and Ali are asking the same question.

In fact, this question is asked by almost everyone I know. We see people get married when we remain single. We see others make more money and have well-behaved kids. Are they just lucky? Have I been dealt a bum hand by some Cosmic Dealer? Or worse, is it all up to me? What torments do I endure to conform to the sexual-industrial complex to secure a partner? What do I have to do to my kids to get them to conform? I have seen my friends weigh the darkness of these prospects. To come back from the brink of desperate extremes they think, *There must be more, some other force at work. But can I rely on the "It" or the "Him" working behind the scenes? Why do other people seem to have it all? What have I done wrong? It feels like an injustice.* But what is the answer?

We are all looking for true north. We need a robust theology of intimacy. "Who is responsible?" is an unanswerable question, but it is a start. And no collection of great circumstances eliminates our ache and struggle with these unseen forces. But if "Who's to blame?" is the best question we have today, we need something better tomorrow. We need a valid reframe and not simplistic platitudes. Our pain knows the difference.

The "God's Will for You" Decoder Club

Jettie made an appointment with me as a college freshman, and I saw her on and off until she graduated. She came to me because she "felt distant from God." She was a devout Christian. She always wore a cross necklace and a WWJD bracelet. I could see she was intelligent, and we would often find ourselves on rabbit trails about unique Scripture interpretations or the role of the Grand Inquisitor in Dostoyevsky's *Brothers Karamazov*.

Jettie's reason for seeing a chaplain was not unique. A perceived distance from God or spiritual stagnation is a common theme, but there is usually a thing under the thing. This was no exception with Jettie.

Over time, as I kept asking questions to pinpoint the source of her frustration, I found something I did not expect. Jettie's problem was not that her spiritual life was stagnant or needed refreshing. I discovered that Jettie had never had a boyfriend and she desperately wanted one. She had also devised that God would bring her a boyfriend once "her life was right." But having her life "right" was a puzzle of endless possibilities that God had not clearly revealed to her yet. In her studiousness, she had devised a kind of spiritual lab where she would try to refresh her life with tireless devotion to God in order to crack his code for her. She would know when she had "got it right" because she would finally find a boy who liked her back and was willing to date her. She could not understand why all the boys she had liked had never liked her back. She surmised that God must be behind it all, withholding these affections because he wanted her to be "better." He seemed reluctant, though, to enlighten her as to what state of devotion she must achieve to crack the lock on this romance vault. She sought me out to help her find this next level of piety because she was frustrated that her own attempts had "not pleased God enough." Also, she was desperately lonely and lovesick.

Jettie's problem is not unique. And our pastoral approach to others in her situation has not been unique either.

I have observed many ministers, upon hearing any myriad of frustrations from emerging adults, respond with this question: "Are you finding contentment in God during your season of singleness?" This question reflects several latent dogmas that frame our orientation of intimacy, and we will need to unpack them as we go along. But can we first agree that there is a tendency to place an emphasis on the role of God (or some metaphysical force) in this human struggle with intimacy? We wield assumptions about the state of one's spiritual life like some kind of relational prescription pad. We diagnose a spiritual condition that must be the cause of our relational aches and pains. Yet our interpretations of just how much and to what end are varied and elusive. It is not a very effective practice.

Whether it is more patience, deeper devotion to prayer, "working on yourself" spiritually to "be ready" for God to send a partner, or the age-old stop-looking-and-they-will-come approach, many of us wield our spiritual prescription pads in the hope that this diagnosis will bring comfort and help to the hurting masses. As a minister, I see myself and my colleagues burning a lot of energy on helping people navigate this phantom variable and how much or little it mingles with their own agency and common sense. Christians especially seem to be asking, What is my role and what is God's role in my relationships? How do I explain these desires I have, considering everything I cannot control in my intimate relationships?

We have done some work defining intimacy by looking at what makes for healthy, sustainable, intimate relationships. But we haven't looked at where intimacy comes from. Lurking in this phantom variable are questions unasked about why we seek out others in the first place. Why does Jettie want to date or be married? Why is she lonely? Why do we seek out friendship or decide whether or not to have children? What is driving us and why? Before we can answer these questions or tackle the unique difficulties of intimacy in our own lives, we must locate a theology of intimacy. We must locate our story in the Great Story that is God's work in the world.

Where Does Intimacy Come From?

One fact that is largely undisputed by Christians and non-Christians alike is that, as humans, we need connection to others. As Christians we would say that we are designed for relationship. This declaration is a fundamental premise for the gospel and salvation: a need to be in right relationship with God. Both practically and spiritually, we assent that no human is an island, and we all require relationships. Yet the simple statement that we are designed for relationship does not necessarily help us answer the dilemma of a phantom variable and our own agency. It does not tell us whether we are called to singleness or marriage or whether we should have children. In fact, once this fact of our humanity is acknowledged, it does little else for us at all in navigating our own desires and struggles.

I propose that *we are not simply created for relationship generally but intimacy specifically.*

How do we know this? Both human science and theology concur that a desire for intimacy is part of the universal, lifelong human condition. The field of human psychology is a natural first stop to show how research backs up our design and need for intimacy. Researchers have provided us copious studies that help us understand that our desire and need for intimacy begins as soon as we enter the world.

Take attachment theory, for instance. This theory begins with the moment of our birth and studies attachment throughout our development. Attachment theory posits that we are born with an innate desire for intimate attachment. We place newborn babies against the skin of a parent shortly after they are born. Starting with the attachment of physical touch, a continuation of new patterns is quickly established in the days, weeks, and months to come. These attachments and connections between the new parents and their baby are critical for healthy development. Even recent studies about "touch starvation" during the pandemic lockdowns reiterate how important physical touch is, not only at birth but throughout our lives. Our desire for intimate attachment is hardwired from birth.

But attachments are more than physical connection. The desire for intimacy is part of our very being. It is here that we locate the harmony of theology and human science. Christian anthropology studies how our spiritual reality informs our physical reality. In other words, our entrance into the world sparks a desire for more than just physical connection. We want to be seen and known.

Every baby comes into the world looking for someone who is looking for him or her. To have a conscious, embodied awareness of being known by God is a necessary feature of the life of loving God, and our awareness of being known by God is measured by the degree to which we are known by each other. This type of hunger abides with us forever.[1]

This is a loaded observation by Curt Thompson that echoes the words of Psalm 139. If we recognize that we are created for intimacy from birth and spend our whole lives desiring it, then the implications lay an important foundation. It is our first move toward true north.

Our desire for intimacy has an origin story. It does not begin at puberty or with romantic love. Indeed, attachment theory supports that all the intimate relationships we develop as we mature are affected by what we learn about intimacy from our family of origin or formative years. Additionally, a desire for intimacy is not something we grow out of. We don't reach our fifties, sixties, or seventies and suddenly wake up one morning no longer needing intimate relationships. Being hardwired for intimacy is part of the whole human condition. Regardless of the era of time, the geography, the family, the culture, or the resources a person is born into, all human beings who have lived or will ever live come into this world "looking for someone looking for us."

So if we are all hardwired for intimacy, how does this inform our pursuit of relationships?

First, it aligns our desires for connection as natural and necessary. Our social development and attachments require intimacy. But intimacy is not simply an outward, social phenomenon; it is essential to our cognitive development as well. "Our middle prefrontal cortex does not develop on its own. It needs the relational interaction of secure attachment—in essence, interaction with other brains—in order for it to eventually function more independently when other brains are not around."[2] And for those of us who are not neuroscientists, the middle prefrontal cortex (PFC) is where decision-making and integration takes place; it is a kind of guide for several cognitive functions including assessing consequences and impulse control. Intimate relationships are key to the healthy development of this part of the brain. I want to point out that this reality is our first clue to a paradigm shift. As we unpack a theology of intimacy, we will find that intimate relationships are not simply being informed by true north, but they are part of the identity of true north. Not just the end, but the means.

Second, we need to widen our conversation about intimacy to more than just romantic relationships. If intimacy is required and necessary for development, then family and friendship, as well as romantic relationships, are required to sustain our engagement with intimacy to the level our human condition requires. Relationships are necessary for the healthy development of the PFC. Family of origin is our first classroom for attachments, but the teen and young adult years provide crucial developmental stages for the PFC. Does this mean if a person does not start dating until their thirties or if they do not date or marry at all, they are doomed to stunted brain development? By no means! The intimate substance of healthy friendship and familial relationships is just as powerful and important. Yet you would not know this if you simply inventoried the sermon series or book topics on Christian relationships. Additionally, it seems cruel and unusual for a loving Creator to hardwire us for intimacy and then confine intimate relationships to just romantic and sexual intimacy.

Third, not all desire for connection is sexual desire. This is a controversial claim. Sex-essentialism operates off the assumption that adults can confidently identify their desire for intimacy as indelibly sexual in nature. Friends are nice, family is important, but what you really need is sex. I touched this nerve early with the claim "I can live without sex . . ." It is not difficult to imagine the temptation to simply reduce any longings of adolescence as primarily sexual. This reduction is the source of several problems identified in chapter two. If I believe that I am entitled to sex via a biological inevitability, then why shouldn't I build a world where sex is fully accessible and available to everyone as desired? If it is a biological necessity, then sex-on-demand is crucial for healthy, human development. Consent might have to go. In fact, many scholars are wrestling currently with this disturbing issue.[3]

Sex-essentialism places our sexual urges at the top of the hierarchy and risks infantilizing non-carnal intimacy. Yes, humans are sexual beings, and our sexual maturity is important physically and psychologically. But we cannot simply equate all intimacy with sexual desire. Indeed, intimacy between a parent and their child must categorically fall into a different arena of desire. To make everything sexual is a wildly dangerous perversion of desire for intimacy. Additionally, if we lack an awareness of our human condition and hardwiring for intimacy, we are in danger of making decisions about relationships that are uninformed at best. At worst, we lack the ability to affirm in ourselves that we are created for intimacy and therefore must take seriously where and how it exists in our lives. If we reduce it to sex alone, we will continue to reap the endless frustrations we currently suffer.

Being hardwired for intimacy is a key component of the human condition. But in our own journey to know and be known, there is still a phantom variable that requires us to locate God in all of this. This is a pivot point in a theology of intimacy: What if being hardwired for intimacy from birth isn't actually the beginning of the story? It is tempting to start with our human condition and search for God in our story, but this puts us at the center. The compass follows us instead of the other way around. As a result, this approach has not been leading us well toward helpful questions or answers.

But what if our story is part of a bigger Story? I'm talking about our human condition, the very fiber of our being, our journey toward being fully developed persons, driven by a desire for intimacy—our story. Perhaps this whole plot came from somewhere else and Someone else. To answer the question of where intimacy comes from, we cannot simply start with our own existence. We must go back to before the dawn of time.

The Cosmic Origins of Intimacy

What is the origin of intimacy? Where does all this start? If humanity is hardwired for intimacy, is there a reason for this that transcends mere biology?

Turning to Scripture, I find myself going further and further back in the narrative to find a source for all intimacy. But my search lands on a fundamental Christian doctrine and confession: the mystery of the Trinity. To engage the Trinity is to encounter a perfect cohesion of three distinct Persons whose internal nature and external acts are undivided. I love the way Fred Sanders describes this:

> The internal actions of the Trinity help us conceive of God in himself as the living and active God, not as a God waiting for a created, historical stage on which to be living and active. They enable a confession of dynamism as part of the divine life. . . . Anchoring the livingness and activity of God in eternal generation [of the Son] and eternal spiration [of the Spirit], Trinitarianism has the necessary resources to declare the external works of the Trinity as undivided.[4]

This core identity, cohesion, and productivity may just seem like beautiful cosmic realities. I know I tend to put some distance between my imagination and the doctrine of the Trinity. But to embrace the dynamic timelessness of the triune God is, in fact, to stare into the torrid nucleus of all intimacy.

Why is this important? Because the origin story of our intimacy does not begin with need and lack. It does not begin with a withholding God. In fact, we have to reckon with the timeless identity of the triune God who lives in a "happy land" of abundance. This constant generation, spiration, and abundance of Father, Son, and Holy Spirit in triune identity and relationship displays the original recipe for intimacy. How do we know this? Because of what happens next: creation. If we look at the opening act of creation, we can gaze upstream at the source of abundance, joy, relationship, power, and delight. In other words, the identity of intimacy within the Trinity is evidenced in the creation story.

The Goodness of Creation: The Original Recipe of Intimacy

Creation is good. It is fruitful. It contains all things bright and beautiful. And the finishing touch is the essential component of relationship. "As the Father, Son, and Holy Spirit have always known fellowship with each other, so we in the image of God are made for fellowship," notes Michael Reeves.[5] This may not be the picture of intimacy that you and I wake up to every morning, but it is the origin. We have to start with the goodness of intimacy in the Trinity and creation because this Story is not lost. As Sanders says, "Simply knowing that the life of God in itself is the liveliest of all lives is a medicinal correction to our sick, self-centered thinking."[6] I invite you to gaze into the unbroken, untainted relationship between God and all things. And when you do, you find the essential presence of intimacy.

These are difficult concepts to get our heads around, but the existence of a relational God whose very identity and timelessness are essential to our understanding of God, ourselves, and the whole of reality, means we must attempt to ground ourselves in this truth. If we were to begin with ourselves and work backward to understand God, we commit a common fallacy of creating God in our own image. There is little that can be known about things that existed before the dawn of time and creation, but the Christian faith and Scripture provide some handholds so that we can be aware of what is essential. *It is important to recognize that intimacy is not an idea we created out of our loneliness, but a gift that is an outflow of the abundance and joy of God's self.* It is not a product of lack. It is not a solution created to remedy a problem. It is not a function: it is bound up in identity.

This timeless, dynamic, self-sufficiency of love and intimacy gives us answers before we can even ask the question "Who is responsible?" We suspect that God is at work, but how? The Trinity and creation are essential chapters, not just to the origin story of intimacy, but to our story. The inner life of God is not just happy for its own sake but also informs the highest ideal of human longing and relationship. Peeking inside the Trinity, humanity gets a glimpse of relationship that is dynamic, vibrant, self-giving, and indelibly connected while also distinct. This glimpse allows us a prologue to the Story of God and our own story whereby intimacy was preeminent, inevitable, and linked immutably to the personhood of a triune God.

And it's a good thing we have this prologue.

I remember the experience of watching the first Lord of the Rings movie with friends who were unfamiliar with J. R. R. Tolkien and who had never read the book. Director/writer Peter Jackson labored over how to provide an informative but time-conscious prologue to the story of the origins of the One Ring and the world of Middle Earth; the presence of the prologue was immensely helpful in allowing non-Tolkien fans to follow and enjoy the movies. Without the prologue, so much of the story would be confusing and odd. The movements of Frodo and the other characters had to be framed in the larger story that gave meaning and context to their stories.

We have our own stories. Jettie is driven by her ache. She can't control all the variables required for her to end up in a reciprocal, romantic relationship. She believes in a God who loves her and is invested in her life, but her efforts to work out this perceived system of God's loving intervention is based on . . . what? Is this how God works? To answer these questions, Jettie must go back to the Story that frames and gives meaning to her own story.

All our stories and lives are part of a larger story of human history. In it are events of progress (or regress) and a spiritual history that tells us both about ourselves and God. The prologue of the "happy land" of the Trinity sets the stage for this history. Act 1 is creation. And creation is, in summary, good.

The divine poem of creation in Genesis 1 and 2 paints a picture of the goodness and outflow of God's very identity. Being the triune God, in relationship with God's self, this identity is bound up with threads of intimacy. But then, humanity is created. What does the intimacy of the Trinity have to do with our human relationships? When we zoom in on the creation of humankind in Scripture, we discern essential and significant components of intimacy.

Enter Human Relationships

As the triune God created humanity "in our image," the origins of humanity were bound up in the threads of intimacy. Creating human creatures, not from loneliness or lack, but from abundance and pure freedom, is one of the most important realities for the identification of intimacy. Curt Thompson calls it a "beauty for which we were destined before the foundation of the world. Beauty that begins and ends with God and our relationship with him and each other."[7] The extension of intimate relationship is both the means and the ends by which this divine beauty is realized. It is not a simple accessory or adornment. Beauty is "a necessity not merely for flourishing but for our very survival."[8] Before everything fell apart, before sin entered the world, before everything was tainted and our identity became vulnerable to lies, we see a world of life-giving beauty, poured from the very identity of God and manifest in relationship.

The very first declaration that something is "not good" (Gen 2:18) signals the primacy of relationship in the human story. It is more than just a nice touch. The role of intimate relationship is cosmic and primal. It is not simply the ordering of human procreation. It is the first cry of salvation echoed through all of Scripture: "God has created universally for all people to be drawn to Him by also being drawn to each other," says C. S. Lewis.[9] Our desire for intimacy is pointing back to a reality whose origin story resides in the poem of creation: who God is and who we are. It is the Story that defines all stories.

But I don't often think about that.

Relationships were immensely important to me as a young adult and took up a lot of my mental and emotional bandwidth. But despite the time and attention I gave to relationships, I never really thought about why I put energy into going on dates. On the one hand, we pour so much time and energy, taxing ourselves emotionally, physically, psychologically, and financially into seeking out and maintaining intimate relationships. On the other hand, my emerging adults routinely affirm that asking big-picture questions about what is driving them is uncommon. So even with our focus on relationships, in some ways, we are sleepwalking. We are like actors reading teleprompters, seldom pausing to ask questions or understand what this whole play is for or why we live this role out on this stage.

We broach the threshold of these concepts when we sense those moments of perceived injustice. When things are not working out in our relationships and circumstances, we begin to wonder about God and the role of faith in our loneliness or frustrations. But we mustn't stop there. As we cross the threshold where our story and the Story of God come together, our questions can change and draw us deeper. Where does intimacy come from? Why do I crave it? Where is God at work in my desires?

We must ask these questions because they will lead us forward in our own story by leading us back to the identity and mission of God. But these new questions will also rouse us from our sleepwalk. They will lead us back to a story of ourselves where our identity, value, and purposes are not random products of meaningless events. In discovering the heart of God, we learn who we are. *When we learn that our desire for sex, companionship, friendship, family, and deep connection is an essential component of the Story of God and Christ's redemptive work in the world, we read the very pages that will tell us who we are.*

If we try a thought experiment, we could imagine a god who could have made us purely autonomous beings whose need for each other is solely economic and cooperative. In this scenario, we can treat relationships as we sometimes treat them now: products to consume for our own satisfaction. Something to simply fill the hole in our lonely lives. But being a triune God, whose very existence is a constant dynamism of intimacy and creative energy, it makes sense that, upon creating humanity, he made us so that we would desire and need one another as we image the very relationship God has with God's self. And from there, all types of relationships are made possible. Did you ever wonder why the historic evolution of human society contains layers of relationships including family, marriage, and friendship? Where did these constructs come from? These relationships did not happen by accident. They have sprung from the imagination of a relational, triune God.

The creation story also contains one subtle but important reality. The connection between the relationship of the Trinity to the flesh-and-bone, dust-and-ash of humanity reveals God's immanence. It is tempting to overspiritualize the fundamentals of Christian relationships. It is popular to point to the transcendence of God and his otherness to anchor the need for modest, chaste, well-behaved relationships. But let's beware of any attempts to overlook the natural and important truths of a personal God extending intimacy into created humanity. In fact, scholar Michael D. Williams observes:

> Though he is the transcendent one, utterly distinct from his creation, for us to enjoy his presence, he must and does choose to enter our world. . . . We never have the feeling that God does not fit in the world, that his appearances are out of place, that he is fundamentally a hermit who dislikes contact with human beings or creation. . . . There is no vague spiritual awareness here, but a tangible experience, an overwhelming one.[10]

Christ-followers often get tripped up on this mystery of transcendence and immanence. We can live lives that tend toward extremes of tedious materialism that forget the inbreaking of the spiritual, or we become Gnostic priests who treat relationships like some spiritual pinnacle of success where we will finally conquer our bodies altogether. But Genesis begins with a theme that reverberates throughout the whole of Scripture: God is transcendent, and God is near. Both realities are essential to understanding our orientation in intimate relationships. We must resist the temptation to overspiritualize or overmaterialize our theology of intimacy.

God Goes First: The Perfect Vision of Vulnerability, Mutuality, and Self-Giving Love

Creation not only tells us why intimacy exists and how, but it gives us a vision for what healthy intimacy looks like. We find an intimacy that is abundant, loving, intentional, and vulnerable. Vulnerability is not first and foremost a result of the fall. In fact, Thompson says, "It begins in the beginning, where we are introduced to a vulnerable God. . . . Vulnerability is not just a random state of neediness or openness to danger. It is built into the cosmic fabric of the world to provide the opportunity for discovery and creation, and for the emergence of beauty and goodness."[11] Intimacy is an act of self-giving love. It is a testament to both its self-giving love and vulnerability that intimacy includes communication and making oneself known. The triune God goes first to show us the way, as Maria Boccia writes:

> Thus, the human capacities for attachment derive from and are grounded in God's existence as three persons in loving relationship and communication of that love to us in both experiential and propositional knowledge. We love because God is love and experiences perfect love in the community of the Trinity and because "He first loved us" (1 John 4:19 NRSV).[12]

Oddly, this first vision of intimacy also contains mutuality. But how can a relationship between God and humanity be mutual? It isn't. Both Aristotle and C. S. Lewis puzzled over this possibility. Each of them concluded that because a god is so very other, there can be no mutuality in a relationship between humans and gods. And in a way, they are right. Humans are not God, and they can never be categorically mutual.

So what kind of mutuality exists in the intimacy displayed in creation? One that exists within the Trinity and is gifted to humanity in how we relate to each other. Boccia observes, "The Trinitarian view of mutuality and self-giving love both explains and motivates human relationships. Thus, contrary to the psychological models, human relationships are derived from the Trinity's mutual relationships."[13] As a result, the revelation of mutuality and freedom in the Trinity challenges individual, entitled autonomy. The Trinity's mutual love of Father, Son, and Holy Spirit defines for us the balance of interconnected love and freedom.

That we are hardwired for intimacy harkens back to an origin story of intimacy that yields the eternal goodness, beauty, and abundance that existed before the dawn of time. It shapes our definition of ourselves and our relationships in light of God's identity and freedom. The love endowed to us through relationship in creation is a beautiful mystery. C. S. Lewis describes it as "a river making its own channel, like a magic wine which in being poured out should simultaneously create the glass that was to hold it."[14] *Both our ability and need for intimacy and others is created by and from a God whose self contains everything necessary and important for us to have both relationships with him and with each other.*

And this would be a nice place to pause. It would be lovely to have Jettie close her eyes and bask in a vision of healthy relationships with God and others that feed each other like the endless garden of good fruit.

But this is not the whole story. Jettie knows it. And sure enough, this perfection does not last longer than the third chapter of Genesis where it all goes suddenly wrong. But this is yet another essential part of the Story, if we are to learn how to live as people created for intimacy in this world.

Deceit, Sin, Fear, and Shame

WHY WE CAN'T SEEM TO MAKE GOOD CHOICES

My first response to the limitations of my love is always the same—to
try harder. I pray for love with more fervor. And I try to love with more
diligence. But nothing seems to change. Then I recall that once again I
have got it all backwards. God doesn't want me to try to become more
loving. He wants me to absorb his love so that it flows out from me.

DAVID G. BENNER

In you, LORD, I have taken refuge; let me never be put
to shame; deliver me in your righteousness.

PSALM 31:1

I love the book *The Neverending Story*. If you are old like me and remember
the classic cinematic hit of the 1980s, then you know at least the first half
of what is in the book. What strikes me every time is the way the theme of
story is used as a larger concept. We see a lonely little boy trying to escape
from his distressing life in the pages of an intriguing book. We follow his
story and are, ourselves, pulled in by the tension of whether the land of
Fantasia and all the wondrous creatures will be destroyed by The Nothing.

At the pinnacle moment, when The Nothing is about to wipe out the very
last bits of Fantasia, Atreyu, the hero, reports to the Childlike Empress that

he has failed his quest to defeat The Nothing. On his journey, he discovered that the only salvation was that a human child gives the Empress a new name. But as the Empress assures Atreyu that he has, in fact, succeeded in bringing a child to them, Atreyu is shocked and dismayed. He concludes that the quest he endured was all for naught if the Empress was already aware of how to save Fantasia. But she assures him: "All your sufferings were necessary. I sent you on the Great Quest—not for the sake of the message you would bring me, but because that was the only way of calling [him]."[1]

I touched on the significance of story and how the telling of an intimate, triune God who creates the world locates intimacy in the metanarrative of Scripture. But we can still feel detached from a story. Like the lonely boy Bastian, we may pick up a book to escape pain or boredom. He never imagined that the story he was reading was set in motion on a collision course with him and his world.

The Childlike Empress explains to Atreyu how the boy, Bastian, could only come to them by the power of story: to enter into the sufferings and victories of the hero, to learn what can only be learned by engaging a story, and to do this without compulsion, as a free agent. "Because he had seen you creatures in your true form, he was able to see his own world and his fellow humans with new eyes. Where he had only dull, everyday reality, he now discovered wonders and mysteries."[2] Bastian can't believe it, and as he reads their conversation, he dares to wonder if he and his story could possibly be part of their story as well.

Perhaps, in our canon of relationship advice, we have not been diligent to point out that the story of the gospel is the Story that locates and orients intimate relationships. But the familiarity of the Story for many of us is the very thing that allows us to take it for granted. Like Bastian, we have not yet dared to dream that this Story has anything to do with *our story*. In fact, if Jettie were here, she might roll her eyes and say, "I know, I know." She grew up on Scripture. She's learned about creation, the fall, the cross, the resurrection, the church, and so on all her life. She didn't come to my office for a Sunday school lesson.

But she didn't come for advice about her love life either.

You might remember that Jettie came to talk to a chaplain about her stagnant spiritual life. Jettie didn't know she was trying to work God into helping out her love life. In fact, until we dug down into the heart of her questions, she wasn't aware of the connection at all. She just thought she needed some professional guidance on how to boost her faith walk. The intersection of her faith and the nagging frustrations of her romantic desires had never occurred to her. She was sleepwalking like the rest of us.

Jettie had created a story about her life: "I need to work harder at my spiritual walk so I can please God." But underneath was the real story, a story with more pain and frustration than the first story dared to admit. Instead of jumping to answers and practical applications for a more robust discipleship, we paused long enough to become curious about what was behind the first story. This clarity is important because the stories we tell ourselves paint a picture of our perceived identity and value, and also how we understand the identity of God.

She was waiting for God to "fix" her atrophied love life because she had written a different story about who God is and how God operates in the world. She did not see the invitation to bring her desire and loneliness into the scope of the gospel. This is because, though she could cite the truths of the gospel chapter and verse, she couldn't see what any of it had to do with her relational woes. Jettie, like the rest of us, required some curiosity and clarity so that she could be honest about her own story. As followers of Christ, this clarity is provided by God's Story. But the Story told on the pages of Scripture is not simply a tool or a lens by which we re-center ourselves and ask *what does Scripture have to say about my life?* Rather, like Bastian's collision course with Fantasia, our story and the Story are threaded together in a dynamic, relational reality.

It is not insignificant that the majority of Scripture is narrative. Scholars have taught us that the whole arch of Scripture is the Story of God, and that even all the small stories are part of the larger Story. We might not readily see what all this has to do with side-hugs, roommates, blind dates, or sex, but to apply a theology of intimacy to the questions and issues plaguing our relational lives, we must recapture the Story that orients all stories.

If the Scriptures remain simply distant facts like a user-manual we can only attempt to apply to our lives, we might end up with copious books and lessons about how the Bible helps you "win" at relationships or "date successfully." But the extrapolations will be thin and varied. Because, instead of anchoring in the gospel, they will be paper houses built on proof texts about godly behaviors. They will contain some good advice but will not make us more mature Christians.

What happens in this familiar Story is ultimately what allows us to make sense of God, our world, and ourselves. Even the broken parts.

Naked and Unashamed

They were naked and knew no shame (Gen 2:25). I always thought it was a peculiar thing to mention the shameless nakedness at this point in the creation narrative. It is the hinge that moves us from the perfection of God's creation to the calamitous sin of the fall. What follows is act 2, a tale of deceit, sin, fear, and shame. The human creatures, believing a lie, rebel against God's commands and sin enters the world (Gen 3:1-6). They hide, they blame, and as God's words detail, their relationships are broken (Gen 3:7-13). The explanation and nature of the curse outlines a distortion and disruption of the humans with each other, with the natural world, with their origins, and with the movement of evil in the unfolding history of their offspring (Gen 3:14-19).

As their story continues, we see that the world still contains much of the good and beautiful that was gifted in creation. Adam and Eve marry and have children. Relationships and intimacy continue. There are joys and victories, but all is tainted by sin. Evil invades everything good, and even the beauty of the world becomes shadows pointing to a former glory. The grand intimacy endowed by the Trinity to the world is now mingled with evil and broken by sin.

But no one really has to tell us this. Even those who do not profess Christianity will tell you that some of the best and worst things in the world coexist. Relationships bring the greatest joy and worst heartbreak of our lives. The goodness of creation and the brokenness of the fall endue a narrative that makes sense of this paradox.

This co-mingling of beauty and sin also means that we cannot reduce a theology of intimacy to simple behavior modification.

Stop dating losers.

Find better friends.

Make better choices.

Pre-engagement rings? Stop it.

It's not that simple. When I speak about relationships, I walk my students through the diagram of healthy relationships.

I walk them through all the variables and watch as they take notes about the building blocks of healthy intimacy. I tell them, "Just prioritize these things and find someone else who does that as well, and you can have healthy, intimate relationships—"

Then I pause. For one sober moment we all realize that while we have all these scientifically proven elements of healthy relationships, somehow, this isn't enough.

If all it took was for us to know the good that we need to do and do it, then we could close out the self-help industry and simply live good lives. But we don't. Simply being told to behave well and how has never made a lasting change. Why? Why can't we just stop it? Why can't we just do better?

Not to leave my students in suspense, I then add: "But we don't do this, do we? If this could be plugged in, then all we would need are some good practices and reasonable common sense. So what's the problem? Why don't we *just do* this?"

I walk to the board and over top of the diagram, I write in big, smearing letters: SHAME.

When sin entered the world, it did not take long to see the effects. Dissension, murder, exploitation, greed, and violence took hold rapidly in history. But these obvious sins against God and each other were not the only thing at work. Pain in childbirth, toiling with weeds and thorns, cold, heat, hunger, and the like were all results of the fall. The world broke. Additionally, we absorbed the effects of deceit and fear in the form of shame. And this power of shame has been working in us ever since.

What Do You Mean by Shame?

They were naked and knew no shame (Gen 2:25). One of the traits of ancient, near-east storytelling is the intentional presence and absence of details. The poetic telling of the creation and fall with its interchange of mythological and material elements is a brilliant example of theology through artistic genre. In essence, we get a picture of what themes and truths are most important in this part of the Story by highlighting what has been intentionally included. That "they were naked and knew no shame" is not simply a casual observation left in to embellish the scenario with mild erotica. The absence of shame within the context of nakedness creates significant contrast against the actions that immediately follow the fall. It illuminates the root of our problem with relationships (and ourselves).

But what is *shame*? Modern studies have helped us define the presence and effects of shame in our lives. Shame is something we can feel before we can even name it. This occurs in parts of our brain that construct emotional narratives. Curt Thompson explains that "we first develop a felt sense of shame rather than a rational explanation of a series of events."[3] Like our desire for intimacy, the absorption of shame begins so early that the two find themselves coexisting in our psyche long before we can name them.

Translating this to our theological frameworks is crucial. The topic can be difficult for us who are Christian practitioners because shame, guilt, and conviction have been used interchangeably in our English language resources. Biblical commentaries, translated Christian classics, and even our English Bible translations have often used shame, guilt, and conviction synonymously.

I am indebted to Brené Brown and other researchers who helped parse the language of shame and guilt in order to bring clarity to these different spiritual realities. While these more recent enumerations are not fixed rules of biblical linguistics, they are helpful for our purposes, and I will outline them here for our continued use. In summary, *guilt* and *conviction* are used to identify the proper and good responses to our own contributions to a broken world.

If I am insensitive to my husband, it is right and good for me to feel convicted about that. If I go on a bender and burn your house to the ground, I should feel guilt. After all, I am responsible for a good deal of pain and injustice you must now endure. Guilt and conviction are good (even though they do not feel good). But they are only good because of where they lead: to repentance. The act of repentance in the Christian tradition is a movement toward freedom and healing. It is the first step that allows for the possibility of forgiveness, and even reconciliation. There might be a need for reparation (if I burn down your house, I should repair it), but this process is the road back. And even if reconciliation is not an option, the powerful effects of grace are transformative and cannot begin without acknowledgment that is couched in guilt and conviction.

So how do we identify shame in light of guilt and conviction? Initially, the feelings are identical. Guilt, conviction, and shame all seem to manifest in the exact same way. The difference lies in the response that follows the feelings. Our feelings of guilt lead us to a crossroads. They can lead us toward repentance and restoration, or they can go a different way and morph into shame. Our ability to acknowledge sin, take responsibility, confess, and repent is a hallmark of rightly ordered conviction. But shame can tug at us and lead us away from gospel restoration.

Shame weighs us down like an anchor. It isolates us. Shame's hallmarks are defensiveness and dismissiveness. Shame justifies and digs in its heels. Shame accuses and blames. Shame requires us to sacrifice others to protect ourselves. In contrast, guilt and conviction allow us to sacrifice our pride for the sake of others and our own healing. Why does shame behave this way? "The difference between shame and guilt lies in the way we talk to ourselves. Shame is a focus on self, while guilt is a focus on behavior."[4]

In summary: Guilt says, "I *did* something wrong." Shame says, "I *am* something wrong."

This subtle but significant difference is the tension point between actions and identity. If my identity is in Christ and I am set free by the cross and resurrection, then I am free to own my mistakes and be a vessel of grace and restoration. But if my identity is in question, the accuser has an opportunity to diminish me. In essence, I become the sum total of my mistakes. I'm no longer a messy, beloved person who failed to be a good friend when I overlooked your birthday. Shame tells me that I cannot recover from my mistakes because I *am* a bad person, hence a bad friend, so I should just stop trying. Shame can cause us to withdraw but also lash out. It's not like *you* were the first person to wish *me* a happy birthday last year. Who has a birthday in the middle of the playoffs anyway? Rude.

Curt Thompson helps us again here:

> Researchers have described shame as a feeling that is deeply associated with a person's sense of self, apart from any interactions with others; guilt, on the other hand, emerges as a result of something I have done that negatively affects someone else. Guilt is something I feel because I have done something bad. Shame is something I feel because I am bad. In fact, when in its grip, it is quite difficult for us to separate ourselves from the shame that we are feeling.[5]

Shame's evil connection to our sense of identity is dangerous and incredibly important for us to locate. "They were naked and knew no shame," but why mention this? Yes, sin, fear, and deceit are all present in the account of the fall. Additionally, sin, fear, and deceit are dangers to our relationships. But there is an important reason why shame is identified as the variable that contrasts the goodness of God's creation with the effects of sin entering the world. In essence, to examine the fall's effects on our relationships, we can't simply reduce it to the concept of sin. There is intent behind the statement, "they were naked *and knew no shame*" instead of "they were naked *and did not sin*" (emphasis mine).

If we examine the events of the fall, we do not find the word *shame*, but we find clues of its presence. Deceit, sin, hiding, blaming, and fear are all manifest in shame. Before their eyes were opened by their act of sin, the first humans bought a lie that targeted the core of their identity. No weak or conspicuous lies were used by the enemy; true deceit is the mark of a lie that works. A lie that sells is the lie that finds our vulnerability. Before the act of disobedience, the first humans needed to doubt their own identity in light of the trueness and identity of God. They lost themselves even before the first fruit was plucked because they already believed that God was holding out on them. It's as though it was all up to them to fulfill their destiny. But when their eyes were opened, the major casualties were all of their relationships—with themselves, with each other, with the world, and with God.

Shame and Intimacy: Our Human Condition

Our intimate relationships contain both the goodness of creation and the brokenness of the fall. In each of us, there is an internal battle we may not even be aware that we are fighting. But the effects tell the tale.

For example, my college students are exhausted. This chronic state of tiredness arises naturally from the pace of college life. But something my students do not anticipate is the weight of their newfound freedom. Most of them came to college to study hard, work hard, and achieve. But they also discover that under those expectations are another set of expectations that college is supposed to be a fun and formative time. Students find themselves torn between choices that often oppose each other. If they choose to cut loose and enjoy themselves, they suddenly end up stressed under the pile of assignments they have to do. On the other hand, if they are driven by the constant drumbeat of achievement, they are liable to fill every waking moment with class, studying, internships, and work. Most struggle to find a balance. The amount of energy and whiplash between these opposing priorities often finds them exhausted by midterm.

In our relationships, we suffer from a similar malady. Below the surface, we often fail to detect the enormous amount of energy we expend to manage our shame as we bounce back and forth between inviting healthy intimacy and pushing it away. This wouldn't make sense if not for what we learn from our "first parents" and what happens to them after the fall. Their relationships become an exhibit that reflects back to us our own human condition.

There is a larger cosmic reality "that in every one of these relational instances, the fire of God's Spirit is burning in a way that reflects what the biblical story contends is, ultimately, our desire for God and our desire to be desired by him—albeit without shame as part of the conversation."[6] We are hardwired for intimacy from birth, but the presence of shame in our lives rings true the effects of the fall. Something in our pursuit of intimate relationships is broken.

Research shows that humans are able to absorb shame at a very early age. Before we acquire the use of language and other faculties that help us make sense of our world, our brains have been able to detect those sensory-affective tones and emotional shifts that encode shame into our neural-networks. And just as a desire for intimacy affects all humans and lasts the whole of our lives, so does our struggle with shame.

This is our human condition. Like my college students, we burn energy attending to the demands of both intimacy and shame, and we are largely unaware of this ongoing effort. Like programming that is running in the background of a computer, draining the battery, this part of our human condition is evidenced in our exhaustion and frustration, but it's not always clearly diagnosed in our own lives. To help us with this, let's look at how intimacy and shame pull us in opposite directions.

Shame Is the Enemy of Intimacy

Every type of intimate relationship requires certain practices and attention to be healthy and sustainable. Just being told the right thing to do does not necessitate that we will do it. Something is always at work tugging us away from the good and beauty we crave. To identify this in our lives, here is a basic list of how both our desire for intimacy and our struggle with shame pull us in opposite directions.

Intimacy requires connection; shame requires isolation. Not to be confused with the healthy practices of solitude or boundary setting, the type of isolation shame brings is one that threatens the closeness and connection of our intimate relationships. Thompson explains: "Our problem with [shame] is generally that we tend to respond to it by relationally moving away from others rather than toward them, while experiencing within our own minds a similar phenomenon of internal disintegration."[7]

Intimacy requires being seen and known; shame requires hiding and secrecy. Just like our ancestors in the Garden of Eden, the need to hide is shame's instinctual response to sin. We do not want to be seen or known. Shame indicts us with accusations telling us we are better off if no one knows what we did or who we truly are. "Shame cannot survive being spoken. It thrives on secrecy, silence, and judgement," Brené Brown reminds us.[8] Hiding is shame's response to the sins we commit, like in the fall, but it is also shame's response to sins others commit against us. We can even feel shame for things that had nothing to do with us or our behaviors.

The woman in the Gospels who suffered from years of bleeding is healed when she touched Jesus' cloak (Mt 9:20-22; Mk 5:25-34; Lk 8:43-48). Her illness made her unclean in her religious and social community, causing her shame even though it was no fault of her own. And the effects of shame linger as she slips back into the crowd. Jesus' call to know who touched him was not to expose her in shame—but to cure her shame by being seen and known and called a daughter by her Savior. He completes the miracle of her healing. The bleeding had stopped, but her identity was still at stake. He called her forward so that she and everyone there could witness the restoration of her personhood.

Intimacy requires truth and trust; shame requires deceit and fear.
The hiding and isolation shame requires is facilitated by lies and fear. Henri Nouwen writes about how "fear is the great enemy of intimacy. Fear makes us run away from each other or cling to each other but does not create true intimacy."[9] When God asked our first parents why they were hiding, they did not respond that they were ashamed. They said they were afraid. Shame thrives when we live in a "house of fear." Fear lashes out because it sells us a lie that we need to protect ourselves and that no one will do it for us. Trust breaks down in the scene of blame that follows the first humans' fearful hiding. Their relationship disintegrates before our eyes as the curse reveals itself before it is ever articulated by God. This fear is fed by the lies that have been lodged against our very sense of self. The deceit of shame attacks our identity. Intimacy says: I love you. Shame says: you don't deserve to be loved.

Vulnerability: The Currency of Intimacy

One of the joys and frustrations with intimate relationships is that they require vulnerability. This was a sticking point in my own dating life. After enduring a painful, failed engagement early in my young adulthood, I remained particularly cautious even years later. I had been in a wonderful relationship for almost two years with Mike, the man I would eventually marry, but I kept him at arm's length. It was a long and difficult journey for me to learn that our relationship could never develop into anything close to engagement because I kept our great love story in the safe stage of limited risk. "No passion without risk" became a motto of our marriage to commemorate an important lesson that I almost learned too late.

"I believe that vulnerability—the willingness to show up and be seen with no guarantee of outcome—is the only path to more love, belonging, and joy," Brown observes.[10] We can't move forward in intimacy without exposing our vulnerabilities. This is why trust and vulnerability must walk together as we mature through our relationships.

My students are awkwardly learning this balance of vulnerability and trust building. Sometimes they jump in and get extremely vulnerable, physically or emotionally, with someone before learning if they are trustworthy. Other times, they get caught in an endless loop of withholding despite evidence of trust. These parallel rails can be difficult to manage in the best of relationships, but with young people still emerging into maturity, the journey can be lopsided. If only one person is sharing themselves, it creates a power differential in the relationship. One person gets to stockpile ammunition and the other person is left exposed.

Just because vulnerability is risky does not mean that we should live in fear of it. If a relationship goes well for many years, we risk being very seen, very known, and potentially very exposed. But if communication and trust-building behaviors of attention, curiosity, self-giving love, reciprocity, commitment, and mutuality are part of the relationship, it creates safety for everyone involved to enjoy the intimacy that comes with being deeply seen and known.

I believe this is why nakedness is mentioned with being unashamed in Genesis.

Nakedness is not simply a state of undress but signifies the full measure of vulnerability. To be naked and unashamed in the full realization of God's created goodness is the joy and safety of being able to be fully seen and known in all our vulnerability. Thompson affirms this:

> I would suggest that shame's mention—juxtaposed to humankind's nakedness—is significant not simply because of what follows but also, and perhaps mostly, because it is primal to what follows. The vulnerability of nakedness is the antithesis of shame. We are maximally creative when we are simultaneously maximally vulnerable and intimately connected, and evil knows this.[11]

After the fall, vulnerability becomes the battlefield on which shame and intimacy wage war. Referring back to the list of opposites about shame and intimacy, it becomes evident how the tug of isolation and connection, hiding and exposure, deceit, fear, truth, and trust are all fighting in our hearts and being played out in our relationships. In some ways, we are just trying to be careful and protect ourselves. Vulnerability is nothing to take lightly and when we allow ourselves to be too vulnerable too quickly without the progression of trust, we leave ourselves open to a world of pain and danger.

This is why a culture that wants all the benefits of intimacy without any work or risk actually risks so much more than it bargained for. As a result, being negligent of the risks of vulnerability can lead to some devastating trauma. I have seen this over the years with my emerging adults. Confined by the rigidity and shame of purity culture, they swing toward licentiousness in an effort to course correct their legalism. But instead of bringing freedom, their misadventures often bring a new kind of shame that is coupled with trauma and heartbreak. Neither purity culture nor hookup culture hold the answers because neither are considering the truths laid out in the gospel that tell us who we are and how this is evidenced in our intimate relationships.

C. S. Lewis warns us of being overly cautious of the risks of vulnerability:

> If you want to make sure of keeping [your heart] intact you must give it to no one, not even an animal. Wrap it carefully round with hobbies and little luxuries; avoid all entanglements. Lock it up safe in the casket or coffin of your selfishness. But in that casket, safe, dark, motionless, airless, it will change. It will not be broken; it will become unbreakable, impenetrable, irredeemable. To love is to be vulnerable.[12]

So how do we manage this risk and experience healthy intimacy in a world broken by sin, fear, deceit, and shame? Are we doomed to have shame continuously gnawing at our efforts toward intimate relationships like a parasite we can't expel? Has the fall tainted everything to the point that our only good news is that someday we will be swept off to glory and be with the Lord once we die?

No.

At the last moment, right before The Nothing consumes the last bits of Fantasia, Bastian accepts that his story is part of The Neverending Story and calls out a new name for the Childlike Empress. Then his real adventure begins.

As it turns out, we have only just made it to Genesis 3. The fall was devastating, but not everything good was lost. Something escaped the curse. The triune God, whose very nature overflowed into the world to create beauty and intimacy out of his own identity, was unchanged by the fall. The beauty and goodness of intimacy lived on because it was first and foremost housed in the personhood of the Trinity. And just as it was part of the "happy inner life of the Trinity" that spilled out into creation, the relational nature of God was about to leverage the role of intimacy again in his rescue mission to redeem all things.

Knowing and Being Known Through the Three Intimacy Motifs

The cross has brought not only peace in our relationship to God, but also reconciliation in ruptured human relations.

PETER J. GENTRY AND STEPHEN J. WELLUM

Jesus replied: "'Love the Lord your God with all your heart and with all your soul and with all your mind.' This is the first and greatest commandment. And the second is like it: 'Love your neighbor as yourself.' All the Law and the Prophets hang on these two commandments."

MATTHEW 22:37-40

How a theology of intimacy is presented is just as important as identifying it. There is a temptation to overspiritualize our approach to a theology of intimacy. In doing so it gets sanitized and treated as an academic idea. The nearness and affection of God are reduced to intellectual ideas that inform but do not transform us. On the other side of the scale, however, is the temptation to overmaterialize a theology of intimacy.

One glaring example of this lives in some of our popular worship ballads. In an attempt to capture the closeness of God, modern worship lyrics have walked a line where on one side I am singing these words to God, and on the other I just said these same words to my sweetheart.

Preston Sprinkle wrote a blog about this very issue titled, "Is Jesus My Boyfriend?" In the blog he makes the observation that in an attempt to describe the clear and pervasive intimacy motifs in Scripture, worship songs reduce these concepts to romantic language.[1] So instead of capturing the transcendence and nearness of a relational God, we have lines in several popular worship songs that can make a person feel a bit icky.

There is an indelible connection between our relationship with God and our relationship with other humans. Conceptual language like "knowing" and "being known" represent both transcendent and carnal relationships. It is no wonder that there is a struggle to discuss a theology of intimacy without slipping into the superficial sentimentalities from our modern culture of romance. In my attempt to move beyond these superficialities (and avoid any ick), I will exercise due caution with the language, presentation, and concepts of a theology of intimacy. In seeking out the beauty of gospel-centric, relational motifs in Scripture there is the risk of overrealizing the anthropomorphisms and their application. With that in mind, I invite you to take a close look at the three intimacy motifs in Scripture—parent, friend, and spouse—and why they are important.

There are two objectives that become the guardrails to guide our theological journey. First, a robust theology of intimacy cannot simply be proof texts of relational behaviors. If it is more, let's identify what it is and where it is. Second, the way a robust theology of intimacy functions in our lives is shaped by the gospel. It is significant for both our relationship with God and our relationships with each other.

For example, I played the cello for many years. I love the range of sound and the beauty I could pull out of the instrument. But I didn't invent the cello. Nor can I take credit for how it is designed and tuned to elicit such fabulous tones. The shape and tuning of a cello is a bit like Christian doctrine. Orthodoxy is an alignment of truths that come to us from Scripture and theology under the historic protection and care of the church. If our doctrines are misaligned, like the cello, they will not make the right sound even under a skilled musician.

But the shape and tune of the cello alone is incomplete—a perfectly made cello is purposeless if it is never played. Our doctrines alone, even rightly ordered, are not enough. The triune God on mission through the redemptive work of Christ by the Holy Spirit makes the doctrine sing. The gospel, or redemptive work of the triune God, is similar to the role of the musician. The technique with the bow and fingering, the ability to control the speed and weight of the bow, this brings the well-aligned cello to life. For those of us in Christ, our faith can be summed up in the animation of Christian doctrine by the living, active person and purposes of God in Christ through the Holy Spirit. The instrument is well made and well played.

Yet I can look back at my own engagement with my Christian faith and see a pattern of stagnation and disenchantment. Doctrines can be very impersonal. And even knowledge of God as a living, active, loving God can feel like a distant, elusive reality.

Many of us hunger for an embodied faith that lives and breathes in our daily life. A robust theology of intimacy orients us toward this.

Embodied Faith

Recently, our church has been working together through the practice of grief. Collectively we have experienced grief, but we have been taking even more time to learn the stories and laments of individuals in our congregation who have been sitting with great loss this past year. First, these individuals have articulated the need for a robust theology of grief. To avoid unhelpful platitudes, we all must become students of the Scriptures. Second, these individuals acknowledge the mysterious but significant presence and work of God in their grief. This faith in a loving God animates the doctrines of Scripture that give them hope.

But the greatest lessons we needed to learn as a congregation were not about a doctrine of grief or the nearness of a God who knows our broken hearts. These individuals asked our priest if they could come before the church and share because of the significant need for relationship in their grief. With tear-stained faces they asked us to show up and be present in very tangible ways. Knowing the right doctrines and believing in the Lord as our Savior and ever-present Lord, while essential, do not implicitly embody the truths that shape our lives on this broken piece of terra firma. For these grieving parishioners, the picture of a church caring for each other required spiritual truths lived out by real bodies in intimate relationship. They were begging us to not just know their lives in an academic sense, but for them to be known through the practice of presence and relationship.

A theology of intimacy cannot just be conceptual, but it does require sound concepts. It cannot just be embodied and risk being over-materialized. But like my grieving friends, the role of intimate relationship is not superficial but essential to our lives and our engagement with the person and purposes of God.

So when we locate intimate relationships threaded into the gospel, it is like sheet music for the cellist. The outpouring of intimacy from the identity and purposes of the triune God is intentionally gifted to us because through these gifts we find God and live out the gospel. The music takes the beauty of the well-crafted instrument, brought to life by an embodied, creative, musician, and teaches us how to apply both of those variables to create the music of God's kingdom. Intimacy plays a particular and important role in our lived faith.

In summary, there is a harmony between orthodoxy and orthopraxy, like when a well-made instrument is played by a skilled musician. Until I began this research, I would never have assumed that the role of intimate relationships was so integral to my faith. It felt ancillary, like a serving suggestion. The application of Scripture to our intimate relationships was always presented to me as topical and user dependent. I did not expect my search for a theology of intimacy to land me deep in the center of the fundamentals of the gospel. Woven into how we live, understand, and grow in our faith is a theology of intimacy orienting everything like the notes of music on the page.

Re-centering and recapturing the primacy of the gospel in a theology of intimacy required a starting point that was not simply proof texts and behavior modification. And I'll be the first to admit, this was not easy.

An Elusive Theology of Intimacy

I remember it was snowing outside and I could see it coming down in the wall of windows across from me. I was in Pittsburgh for my second intensive week and I sat in a square with about a dozen colleagues as we worked through our doctoral theses. It was my turn, and I asked the group for help. I had just set out to study a robust theology of intimacy. I believed that Scripture contained such a thing, but I needed to discover where it was and what it was. So I put it to my cohort: Where should I start to find a theology of intimacy? I was glad for the majesty of the falling snow because it made for a lovely distraction from the silence that followed.

But we did try. Suggestions were made. Much of the time we found ourselves pigeon-holed in texts about sex or marriage, but I wanted to understand the spectrum of intimate relationships and not simply marriage. We struggled for close to an hour. I admit feeling a bit unsettled when we realized that even in a room of brilliant pastors and scholars, we struggled to locate a theology of intimacy in Scripture. But I knew it was there. So I continued to search.

I laugh now at how difficult this all was at the start. After close to seven years of research, I'm a bit embarrassed at how the presence of intimacy in the narrative of the gospel eluded me. Like when you notice an odd sound in a song, and you can't unhear it from then on each time that song is played, I can't learn about the gospel without seeing intimacy woven into it. In fact, I cannot untangle a theology of intimacy from the whole of the Story.

I set out to locate a theology of intimacy, and as it turns out, it is everywhere.

The beauty of the gospel is that it lives and breathes in both over-arching and small ways all throughout Scripture. Biblical, theological, and hermeneutical scholars through the ages have shown us again and again how everything contained in Scripture points us to the good news of God's kingdom through the redemptive work of Christ and the Holy Spirit. But God did not only gift us Scripture so that we could learn the gospel through the power of story. *God framed the gospel in the context of intimacy to illuminate it and create a point of powerful connection with our lives.* The tapestry of the gospel story is woven with threads of intimacy.

Like the sheet music giving beauty and context to the design of the cello and the skill of the cellist, intimacy plays an important function in our faith. It is not a passive variable or solely an ethical category. By the end of this chapter, I hope you don't come away saying, "Isn't that sweet of God to care for us like a parent, or spouse, or friend." Intimacy is not mere sentimentality. God is communicating significant truths about God's self and his gospel. Intimate relationships become the avenues of that communication, but there is something more.

By learning God's nature and mission through the framework of intimacy, we are given the foundation for flourishing in all our intimate relationships. Seeking to grasp a theology of intimacy gives us a way toward restoration and healing. Through it, we will find our way home.

Intimacy Is Everywhere: Even in the Way the Story Is Told

After the goodness of creation and the devastation of the fall, God's grand rescue mission goes into effect. As we walk through the main narrative of Scripture and follow the threads of God's redemptive mission, we find intimacy woven in. But intimacy is not simply a theme. It frames and shapes three key aspects of the gospel: restoring, gifting, and abiding. The rest of this chapter is an overview of these recurring themes, and about the ways intimate relationships are how we understand (1) God's self and his gospel and (2) the fundamentals of healthy, sustainable relationships.

Let's begin with a wide-angle lens that orients the arc of Scripture: covenant theology.

I tend to approach the world with an analytical lens, so when I learned about covenant theology in seminary, it did not occur to me for years to come that this way of mapping the Story of God is bound together with an intentional framework of intimacy. For our purposes here, covenant theology is a beautiful way to navigate the inbreaking of God into history. It reveals the mission and character of God by following the string of covenantal promises throughout the entirety of Scripture.

Along with what it contains about the work and nature of God, it is significant to understand that the substance of covenant is intimacy. Henri Nouwen observes:

> Rooted in a bond that existed before and beyond human together-ness, bonds of true intimacy rest in the divine covenant. This is the covenant of God's faithfulness expressed in the promises made to Noah, Abraham and Sarah, Moses and the prophets, and made fully visible in the incarnation of Jesus.[2]

I am often tempted to think of the gospel in merely transactional terms. The gods of the ancient world operated on a more economic system. If Yahweh were just another ancient god, he could still have imparted righteousness to us through the free gift of grace as a transaction from a benevolent higher being. Like other ancient gods, he could have made deals and contracts with mortals that stipulated a tidy exchange of fealty and worship for blessings. But his use of covenant tells a different story and reveals a different God.

Nouwen observes, "A covenant is a relationship, and that sets it apart from a contract. Contracts also contain promises and obligations, but they are impersonal and non-relational. Covenants stand apart from contracts because the promises are made in a relational context."[3] Through covenant, God promises his presence and makes himself and his purposes known. It may be easy to take for granted the power of God's self-communication, but "the knowledge of God in Scripture is primarily a matter of personal intimacy," Michael Williams notes.[4] God invites us to know him, experience him, and join him in the mission. These covenants communicate the ways and work of God. They stipulate promises that deliver from sin, bestow blessing, and invite us into the family of God. Yahweh not only sets himself apart from the ancient gods and idols, but framing his nature and mission in an invitation to relationship places the role of intimacy in the center of covenantal communication. God's covenants are conduits of his message, and they invite closeness.

In other words, covenant marks the path that restores and reconciles us to our Creator. In covenant, God abides and dwells with his people. And God communicates and invites us to a relationship made safe by his self-giving love.

Whether with Noah, Abraham, Moses, or David, God's covenants place him in relationship with his people. This covenantal journey arrives at the ultimate culmination in the incarnation of Jesus Christ. Covenant, unlike contract, is a promise made and kept in the face of infidelity and brokenness. As a result of the fall, human relationships tatter, underscoring our continual betrayal in the face of God's loving covenants. "Yet before, during, and after humankind's broken promises, the promise-making and promise-keeping God is present and will not let the web fall apart," says Michael Horton.[5]

Books have been written about the role of covenant and its unique function as a relational avenue of grace. But I want to see how intimacy through covenants shapes our spiritual imagination. We get a picture of God that is both regal, powerful, *and* intimate; this should blow our minds. Compared with the powerful but distant gods of the ancient world, Scripture provides a very different picture.

It is the indignity of a father who runs out to embrace his prodigal son. It is a mother, dressed in full evening wear, who gets on her hands and knees to comfort her frightened toddler with the warmth of her voice and presence. The God of the cosmos draws near and says, "I am not just here to make a contract. I want to be known by you and I want you to know me." Salvation is not a mere transaction. God's saving redemption allows this closeness because it requires it. The gift is a Person.

Restoring, Gifting, and Abiding: Parent, Friend, and Spouse

Language for God from the earliest accounts has always been striking and revelatory. The timeless and great I AM and the vowelless breath name of YHWH both signal a holy and intangible being. Like the scenes of the throne room in John's Revelation, there is an echo of this majestic awe that prompts mortals and cherubim to cover their faces. These images are true and right and should not get lost in a theology of intimacy.

But something remarkable and a bit shocking happens as early as the book of Exodus when Moses is conveying God's message of deliverance to Pharaoh. God reveals the first intimacy motif: "Then say to Pharaoh, 'This is what the LORD says: Israel is my firstborn son, and I told you, "Let my son go, so he may worship me"'" (Ex 4:22-23). The enslaved Israelites are revealed as the children of the Heavenly Father.

Scripture is full of titles and illustrations for God that are used to convey the nature and mission of this triune God: the Good Shepherd, the Vine, Prince of Peace, the Way, Lion of Judah, a strong tower, and so on. But starting with this reference in Exodus, the narrative of Scripture continues to build momentum on the foundation of three intimacy motifs: family, marriage, and friendship. The triune God uses these motifs over and over again, teaching us to think of him as parent, friend, and spouse.

To zoom in on these motifs and themes, I offer three key passages that fundamentally capture what is echoed in the rest of Scripture: the three motifs in the context of the gospel. We will use Romans 8:14-17 for familial relationships, Ezekiel 16 for marital/sexual intimacy, and John 15:12-15 for friendship. The significance of these three intimacy motifs cannot be understated as they contain not only the identity of God and truths of the gospel, but also the way by which we engage all our human relationships.

How does intimacy restore? For starters, in every motif, the relationship between God and humanity frames a shift in identification that directly correlates with restoration. In Romans 8:14-17, the family motif is used to claim that the people of God are no longer slaves, but children and heirs of God. In John 15:12-15, Jesus says, "I no longer call you servants . . . instead I have called you friends." In Ezekiel 16, we witness a graphic picture of someone helpless, discarded, isolated, and unknown. But this illustration of God's people is then seen, chosen, and ends up in full union and fully known, like a wife to a husband. The work of reconciliation is threaded with major and explicit shifts in identity. Instead of slaves or servants, or being isolated and unknown, in Christ we become children, friends, fully loved and fully known.

Although this is a remarkable reality, as the people of God we have a problem with identity. The stories of Scripture and even our own lives bear witness to the fact that we often revert to an orphan mindset. We see ourselves as discarded, isolated, alone, unseen, and unloved. God's rescue mission includes us being restored, not just to a debt-free status, but into relationship. I have long taken for granted that this relationship is designed to heal my broken identity.

My life was once saved by two friends. They didn't know it at the time, but I had been on a journey into darkness for several years. I had succeeded in isolating myself, concealing my pain, and letting shame, lies, and deceit convince me that I was trash. These two girls were new to town and new to our church. For whatever reason, they turned their sights on me and kept asking me to hang with them. Despite my deep entrenchment, this consistent invitation and their simple, sincere choosing of me was too much. I was drawn into their gravitational pull, and it ended up being the catalyst that changed the entire trajectory of my life. It took me years to finally toss off the mantle of darkness I had let define me, but it began because the very act of being chosen and invited into friendship made me doubt the lies.

The power of being chosen and invited into relationship is one God is wielding with gusto. God relates to us as his children, friends, and spouse; and what's more, he reveals our relationships to be sites of his restorative work. This God who chooses is calling us out of fear, slavery, drudgery, and abandonment. Restoration is a beautiful but messy process. These shifts in our status and identity are available to us even though we will prove unfaithful. The theme of self-giving love deepens our understanding of what is driving this reconciliation, despite our failures.

The power of gifting: A story of relentless self-giving love. When Jesus calls his disciples his friends in John 15, he does so with the knowledge that betrayal is coming. The beautiful picture of union in Ezekiel 16 is about to devolve into infidelity. Scripture extends the intimacy motifs to describe the breakdown of relationship between God and humanity: God as jilted husband, frustrated father, and betrayed friend. The work of restoration is tough in every intimate relationship. It can be a roller-coaster ride of victories and defeats. This is why self-giving love is at the heart of these motifs.

Covenant is distinct in that one party holds fast even in the face of betrayal. If our relationship to God was contractual, then as soon as we failed to meet expectations, he would be well within his rights to no longer meet his obligations. But the covenants made by God bear out that he remains faithful even when we are unfaithful. Love is the power that enables this incredible sacrifice. It is a gift. Love's sacrifice is inviting the hungry to an extravagant banquet and never looking at the bill. Love's gift is not a martyrdom we use to guilt people. It is not an indiscriminate emptying like Shel Silverstein's *The Giving Tree*.[6]

We struggle with this in our human relationships. It is difficult to maintain the balance of boundaries and radical generosity. But gifting is fundamental to intimacy. In John 15, Jesus declares that the highest of all love is "to lay down one's life for one's friends." And he sets out to do this very thing on the cross. God initiates a powerful act of love by choosing us, but then he doubles down. Gifting makes this invitation to relationship sustainable along the journey. Being chosen starts the relationship, but gifting keeps it going.

Choosing is powerful, but it is also easy. Every dating relationship I've ever had started because two people took a risk to choose each other. But only one of those relationships ended in marriage. The others just ended. This was not because Mike was perfect and the other guys were imperfect. But our ability to keep choosing each other every day of our lives (a very tall order considering how messy and broken we are) would only have the hope of possibility if we learned how to love like Christ loves. And Christ is not simply the model but the very embodiment of Love.

The use of the intimacy motifs demonstrates that God's love is invitational, accessible, and a gift of one's whole self. It is invitational due to the affective language used where we are called *sons and daughters*, *bride, beloved*, and *friend*. The terms invite closeness and intimacy. It is accessible because God reveals and discloses himself. Jesus is explicit in John 15 that what makes the disciples friends and not just servants is the access and disclosure of one to another. Love is predicated and accessible because the triune God—powerful and unknowable—is constantly making himself known and revealing his mind, heart, and knowledge in loving communication with his creation.

And this love is a gift of one's whole self because it is given by sacrifice and constancy. Even though Christ's death on a cross was a singular, profound moment in time and space, it cannot be reduced to being the only expression of self-giving love in Scripture. There is a consistent, long-suffering demonstration of God's love that we cannot take for granted in our own definition of self-giving. Sure, I would not hesitate to take a bullet for my older brother; he is my only sibling and there is no question that I would give my life for his if given the chance. But would I commit to being patient and long-suffering with him? Am I amenable to sacrificing chunks of myself at each holiday gathering in order to love him without expecting reciprocity?

"The LORD is compassionate and gracious, slow to anger, abounding in love" (Ps 103:8). The long-suffering and patience of God is evidenced in the use of these motifs throughout the ups and downs of God's relationship to his people. Whatever caricatures we make for God, the language of parent, friend, and spouse is constantly pulling us toward a true north picture that course corrects our misalignment. And if we ever wondered about God's purposes and mission in the gospel, we see restoring and gifting woven together with the ties of intimate relationship. But there is one more theme we cannot escape: abiding.

Abiding: God is with us and in us. These motifs are thoroughly trinitarian. The Son is friend, God is Father, and—though God is also husband—the Holy Spirit is a unifying agent representing, creating, witnessing to, and enacting intimacy. At every turn, the presence of intimacy in Scripture is woven indelibly in the work and person of the Holy Spirit. It is the work of the Holy Spirit that enables believers initially to become lovers, friends, and children of God.

In the family motif of Romans 8, Paul uses this section of the letter to explain the concept of the "law of the Spirit" setting us free and how believers are called to live by the Spirit and not the flesh (vv. 1-8). He writes about the Spirit's work in the life of Christ and how the Spirit enables belonging to Christ (vv. 9-14). Within the midst of a restorative transition of identity and gifting of love, we find the Holy Spirit enabling and witnessing. In the reconciling shift from slaves to sons and daughters, it is the Spirit who enables and is the initiating catalyst for a change of station and identity that humans could not do on their own. The very act of freedom from slavery is attributed to the Holy Spirit.

This third person of the Trinity is not only enabling intimacy, but in a unique way, the Holy Spirit *is* intimacy. The first example of this can be seen in the Holy Spirit's role in the relationship of Jesus to God the Father. Scholars have taken the High Priestly Prayer that Jesus prays in the Garden of Gethsemane to be a

> communion mediated by the Spirit, a mediated intimacy. . . . As the mediator of the intimacy of the Father and the Son maybe we should think of the Spirit, not just in typically Western terms as the one who holds them together, but as the one who, as the mediator of their mutual love, holds them in their distinctiveness as Father and Son and preserves them from an indistinct oneness.[7]

The Holy Spirit's role in the Trinity consists of pure intimacy that binds Father and Son to one another, as well as the Father to adopted sons and daughters through Jesus the Son. The fluidity of presence that the Spirit embodies allows for the mystery of the indwelling to reside in every believer.

One of the greatest gifts and mysteries is the indwelling of the Holy Spirit, union with Christ in us and through us. The gifts and power of the Holy Spirit is a doctrine most taken for granted in our lived theology and one that has also been most abused and distorted. I know friends who can barely talk about the Holy Spirit because of the spiritual abuses they suffered "under the authority of the Holy Spirit" in their local church. Yet a robust theology of intimacy requires us to reckon with a God who is not just near but *in us*.

Because the person of the Holy Spirit and the theme of abiding are too important to gloss over, I want to anchor into these two statements:

1. The way we indulge in the power and gifts of the Holy Spirit should be mediated by the fruit of the Spirit.

2. The deep abiding presence of the Holy Spirit is a concept so transcendent that our material engagement with intimacy can only act as a signpost to the higher reality.

The marriage motif is critical to elevating our capacity to understand a mystical union that happens between disciples and Christ. The motif of God as Bridegroom and us as his bride is a difficult concept that Christians have struggled with for a long time. In modernity, this is where we tend to bring the ick as we seek to understand the role of sexual union in the gospel. Paul has already cautioned us in Ephesians 5:32 that "this is a profound mystery" that is Christ and his church. These shadowlands we live in reveal the limits of these motifs in the ways we think about God. Sex is a powerful, unmatchable display of trust, vulnerability, and self-giving love. It is the closest we can get to having any reference for the kind of cosmic union that transcends our human materialism. Sex is an important signpost that falls short of the transcendent but essential reality of the indwelling of the Holy Spirit.

Nothing could be more intimate than the living, abiding presence of God's Spirit inside his people. The profound idea that God is literally inhabiting his people must remain central to any discussion of a theology of intimacy. Joel Beeke and Paul Smalley explain:

> Christ's union with His body transcends the union between any earthly husband and wife because He lives in His body by the Holy Spirit (1 Cor 6:15, 17; 12:12-13). Christ promised to send the Spirit to dwell in His people, and promised, "I will come to you . . . Because I live, ye shall live also" (Jn 14:17-19).[8]

The Holy Spirit endows us with an eternal essence that is infused into our personhood. Like a lightning bolt being the evidence of an electrical charge coming up from the earth and down from the heavens, the Holy Spirit is the force that links our material selves to an eternal self. "Though we may perish physically in our afflictions, yet we shall live forever, for already we are joined to Christ in His resurrection, and are 'his body, the fullness of him that filleth all in all' (Eph 1:23)."[9]

So in noting that the Holy Spirit is also what is connecting us to each other, we must reckon with the fact that this horizontal connection is as eternal and powerful as what is connecting us to God. The implications of this for our human relationships are astounding, and I will unpack the significance of this in subsequent chapters.

One way we see this played out is that the Spirit facilitates intimacy by enabling candid, intimate communication. How will we ever learn who God is? How can we truly know God's identity, nature, will, and purposes? It must happen in relationship with and through the power of the Holy Spirit. Without the Holy Spirit, this kind of essential communication would not be possible. As Philippians 2:13 attests: "For it is God who works in you, both to will and to work for his good pleasure" (ESV). And just as the Holy Spirit enables a transcendent access and communication between us and our Savior, he is also responsible for a transcendent access and communication in our intimate relationships with each other.

Science Confirms What Scripture Has Told Us All Along

Anyone who has tried to teach Christian content about relationships knows that we struggle to do translation work between the modern world of intimacy and the scant few references to modern relational woes in Scripture. (I mean, would it have killed an apostle to drop in a paragraph about how to make a dating profile? Come on.) But even though we lack directives from Scripture—on how to gently parent a child with special needs, or whether to go to the in-laws or the beach with our time off, or what to do if we are being ghosted after a first date—with a robust theology of intimacy we can discern direct parallels that inform our human relationships. With the gospel themes of restoring, gifting, and abiding couched in the relational invitation of our Savior, the fundamentals of healthy intimacy surface to reveal a familiar framework.

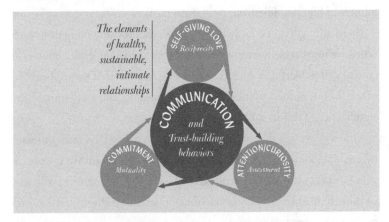

The scientific study of human relationships continues to produce research that affirms and re-affirms the fundamentals of healthy, sustainable intimacy. But if we were paying attention to a robust theology of intimacy in Scripture, we would have discovered for ourselves that the triune God of creation—Father, Son, and Holy Spirit—emulates, embodies, and reveals the very mechanisms for access to the beauty of intimacy.

IN THE DIAGRAM	IN SCRIPTURE
Self-giving love: Involves the giving of oneself in a number of ways.	Self-giving love: God is love (1 Jn 4:8,16); abounding in love (Ps 86:15 et al.); demonstrated on the cross (Rom 5:8).
Attention/curiosity: An orientation toward/ seeking after the other at the outset and sustained over the course of any relationship. Commitment: Choosing to be with another over and over again.	Attention/curiosity and commitment: These are demonstrated throughout Scripture but are most evident in the themes of choosing (Jn 15:16); abiding (Jn 15:4); and God's faithfulness through covenant (Ps 105:8).
Reciprocity: The back-and-forth commitment of giving and receiving. Includes personal investment and exchange of resources (social, material, personal, etc.). Mutuality: Especially mutual acceptance of and respect for one another.	Reciprocity and mutuality: The amount of reciprocity and mutuality in a theology of intimacy is shocking considering the relationship between God and humanity has a drastic power differential. The fact that God invites us to participate in his work and enables us to love as he loves through the power of the Holy Spirit is a marvel. We see this in the journey of our sanctification. Through Christ, we enter a death that leads to life.
Assessment/managing expectations (both together and as individuals): Continually determining the health/success of the relationship.	Assessment/managing expectations: While necessary to navigate intimacy between two broken humans, assessment in Scripture is made possible through the Holy Spirit. With this transcendent means of communication and insight, we can assess our own brokenness and entrust our transformation to the loving process of our Savior.

This table captures a picture of how these themes emerge and are embodied in the person and mission of the triune God. But the foundations of these practices are locked in by *communication* and *trust building* at the center. Now, I could go on and on about how these fundamentals are manifest in Scripture, but I want to offer a few nuggets of examples that I find particularly amazing.

For example, the Holy Spirit facilitates and makes communication possible. The need for healthy, open communication is stated by Jesus in

John 15 as he reveals essential variables for friendship. But being friends with God also requires a standard of obedience that requires knowing God's will. This desire to know God's will is standard practice for Christians but can be a difficult process when we recognize the power differential between us and God. God is all-powerful and can essentially orient our lives in whatever way pleases him. This leaves us feeling vulnerable and exposed. Even though we know God is loving, the power dynamic can be difficult to surrender to. It is like when C. S. Lewis ponders: "We are not necessarily doubting that God will do the best for us, we are wondering how painful the best will turn out to be."[10]

Yet the economy of God has established an invitation to intimacy that allows for our agency and consent that does not diminish his power and sovereignty. Michael Horton notes: "The Spirit is not merely a servant of God. On the contrary, precisely because he is other than God, he can bring the Father's will to pass. And precisely because he is other than the Father, he can do so by working within us to win [and woo] our consent."[11] *God's lovingkindness makes a way for our agency and consent to remain intact even as we surrender our finite limits to his immense knowledge.* The mutuality and reciprocity of intimacy in the Trinity pours out into God's design for us so that we can draw close to a God who is very different from us yet makes himself accessible.

Another example of this is how God uses the intimacy motifs to rescript hierarchies. Again, God is wholly other, eternal, vast, and powerful. In any ladder of hierarchy, God is always at the top. But hierarchies are measures of power differentials and power differentials can make intimacy very difficult. Yet once again, in his infinite wisdom, God uses the intimacy motifs to create a safe and viable invitation for us without diminishing his power in any way.

The family motif is central to framing this power differential without threat of abuse. In Romans 8, the language of adoption and being claimed as sons (and daughters) presupposes a proper and ordered relationship between humanity and God. Galatians 4:6-7 also contains these themes explicitly when Paul notes twice that believers are no longer slaves but are made children and heirs, adopted with hearts that can now cry out "Abba, Father." But in Romans 8:14-17, Paul outlines this transition in more detail: "For you did not receive the spirit of slavery to fall back into fear, but you have received the Spirit of adoption as sons, by whom we cry, 'Abba! Father!'" (ESV).

People are moved from slaves to children because adoption has relocated them out of a realm of fear and into a station of freedom. Both the Galatians and Romans passages use the imagery of slavery and freedom in contrast, moving believers from an unreconciled age of fear because God is judge, to a new reconciled status as children and heirs where God is Father and freedom is central to our new identity. The emphasis on a shift away from fear is key to recognizing that God is presenting as a parent who does not lord their power over their child, but in love wields that power for the ultimate good and freedom of the ones who cannot free themselves. This aligns with the beautiful kenosis passage in Philippians 2:5-8 where God does not diminish his power but through the incarnation of Christ leverages his power in humility for the sake of the other.

In all this, God is drawing us in and building trust so that we can know that even though he is all-powerful, he is also all-loving. Scripture is an oracle of how intimacy can be sought after with principles and virtues that create safe, loving, viable, and sustainable avenues to deepen our relationships. What we learn about God and his gospel through restoring, gifting, and abiding also contains the very fundamentals that scientists have proven again and again to be the way of healthy intimacy.

We cannot talk about intimacy without talking about the gospel. This truth redefines how I approach every person who comes through my door. If intimate relationships are created to draw us to God and his purposes, and if this gifts us the fundamentals for healthy relationships—because we know and love God, and are being known and loved by God—then we have a new framework that is not really new at all. It is just a re-centering of the gospel we have had all along.

Payton and I have been meeting together for over a year. She sought me out for spiritual guidance while discerning whether or not to commit herself to a life of vocational singleness. This would mean that she would not pursue romantic or sexual relationships and instead use the freedom of singleness to devote herself to ministry. These are difficult but beautiful conversations, and I have witnessed her fears, insecurities, hopes, and doubts in this journey. But in our time together—more than the mechanics of relationships, the difficulty of friendships, or the struggle of loneliness—she wants to talk about the gospel. I tear up a bit as a write this because she ministers so much to me in how she clings to a dynamic hope of a God who calls her "Daughter."

Payton is still not sure what road to take, but we never miss an opportunity to remember that she is created for intimacy and no matter what, God will never abandon her to isolation and scarcity. For Payton, these are more than just abstract ideals; they are oxygen. Because of the gospel, being known by God is not a bloodless hope. It is what gives her the fortitude to imagine a life of abundance and intimacy, to know and be known, come what may.

8

Loneliness and the Location of God

*Friendship, I said, doesn't solve the problem of loneliness so
much as it shifts its coordinates. Just as marriage isn't a magic
bullet for the pain of loneliness, neither is friendship. It does,
we hope, pull us out of ourselves, orienting our vision to our
neighbors. But no, I said, it's not enough. It's never enough.*

WESLEY HILL

*By this everyone will know that you are my disciples,
if you love one another.*

JOHN 13:35

Have you ever heard this one: "I just need to be single right now so that
I can focus on my relationship with the Lord"?

If Christendom had a top ten of famous breakup lines, this one would
be at the head of the list. It's the trump card. How do you argue against a
singular reverence for Jesus? It is particularly effective. Who am I to stand
between you and your devotion to our Savior? To want to stay in a relationship at risk to your spiritual health would be selfish. So I can either
appear petty, selfish, and unholy by pushing back against the breakup, or
I can appear angelic and magnanimous, and gracefully bow out.

They get their breakup without any fuss, and the added bonus of spiritual
piety . . . until they pop up two weeks later on the dating apps. (True story.)

But before the hypocrisy reveals itself, we can all agree that there is something off about this breakup tactic. It's tricky because there is absolutely nothing wrong with

- sensing that you need to get out of a relationship,
- noticing and wishing to remedy a spiritual dry spell, and
- attempting to place God above idols in your life.

So why does this still feel icky? I believe that people have genuinely used this line out of a sincere desire to place God first in their life. After all, our relationship with God is the most important relationship of them all. I propose that an off-putting scenario like this has to do with creating a binary between a relationship with God and relationships with others.

The breakup line is just one example of this. But I observe a difficulty in building a culture of discipleship that keeps the focus on God and diminishes the idols that tempt our worship. There is a difficult tug between attempting to turn "quiet times" into the single-minded veneration of a hermit whose whole life is devotion to the worship of God, and normal life with the bills, the schedule, and the demands all seeming to work against a holy life.

This is a temptation to create false binaries in our spiritual life between the "holy things" and the "normal things." The breakup line reveals how this binary shows up in our experience of relationships. We assume that to be in a holy relationship with God, we might have to annex certain relationships with others. But what if our relationships with others were the housing for where we experience God, and intimacy where we learn and live the gospel?

As I have observed, relationships live on a plane both vertical (relationship with God) and horizontal (relationship with others). Here's what we know.

God has provided us with motifs that allow us to engage something familiar in order to learn things that are transcendent. There is context for relationships like family, friendship, and marriage. So when Scripture uses the language and concepts of these motifs to describe how the Lord sees and loves us, we can reference this and say: "Oh! My parents are not perfect, but God is. And I can sort of see what kind of parent God is through his perfection."

The motif of marriage in the New Testament does this explicitly. The author of Ephesians ends the section about husbands and wives by claiming: "This is a profound mystery—but I am talking about Christ and the church" (Eph 5:32). So our human relationships act as a signpost that point to the mysterious, transcendent things of God. We get a framework for how God loves us and is like a parent or a friend or a spouse.

But these motifs are not just symbols or signposts. Our horizontal relationships are not simply broken versions of the perfection of Christ.

Intimacy Is the Enemy of Shame

Back in chapter four, I had a group of students who could not get over the seemingly rigid and graceless way we instruct people to live in relationship. All this talk of purity, modesty, waiting, gender roles, submission, and good behavior did not seem to provide them with a beautiful picture of a relationship to ascribe to; it seemed an impossible standard they were doomed to fail. And if they did fail, the only hope was to repent and then get back on the right track. You may have slept with your old boyfriend but moving forward, just be sure you never sleep with a boyfriend again and there may still be hope for a beautiful marriage someday.

But we messed up.

Looking solely at romantic relationships, I can tell you hundreds of stories from dozens of couples my husband and I have had the privilege to provide premarital counseling for. Whether they followed "the rules" or not; whether they stayed virgins or didn't; whether they adhered to certain gender roles or not; they were all going into these marriages as deeply flawed and broken people. These things did not save them. They did not even necessarily make them better people or better equipped for healthy marriages. In fact, adherence to some of these rules and roles actually made them *less ready* to enter marriage.

They look to us for advice on how to get it right. How can we make good choices, treat each other well, and protect our marriage? How do we get it right?

Just like with my young students navigating roommates, dating, parents, siblings, and friendships, there is certainly some common-sense, practical advice to be had. When Mike and I work with couples in premarital relationships, we do not neglect to help them communicate expectations, figure out chores and holidays, manage money, and practice mutuality and equity. But these fall under a greater thesis that is the heart and soul of the premarital sessions: learning to be grace givers and grace receivers because of the power of Christ's gospel.

These sweet, excited couples are going to mess up. They are going to hurt each other. They are going to be some of the most hurtful people in each other's lives, because the intimacy is so deep in their exposed vulnerabilities. Hurting the ones we love, and being hurt by them, is a major source of shame. When our lives are so deeply connected, we run up against our failures and mess again and again. Shame metastasizes in this loop of guilt and disappointment.

But there is hope! Intimacy is the enemy of shame.

When we counsel these premarital couples, we announce that marriage, like any intimate relationship, is a master class in forgiveness. And it is not just the art of conflict resolution, learning how to make an actual apology, or shedding your favorite evasive maneuvers. The ability to give or receive forgiveness is like exorcizing our own demons. I sense this in myself. There is a part of me shrieking with resistance every time I have to offer or receive grace, because doing this well requires a deep plunge into the subterranean levels of the gospel.

We forgive because we have been forgiven (Col 3:13). But do I really get the weight and reality of that? Do I believe it? Intimate relationships expose my quiet, functional atheism. To have and keep the best relationships in my life, I have to cling to the plank of the gospel like a shipwrecked soul. I have to know it and ingest it again and again.

But praise be to God! I do not just have to go off and figure it out, and then return once I've mastered it so that I can have a healthy relationship. I learn it and absorb it and live it *in relationship*. My intimate relationships are the living, ecological lab where I experience sanctification through the gospel. My spiritual formation is not the result of diminishing my relationships in order to elevate a solo hike with Jesus. My relationships are where I experience Jesus.

For years, I've struggled with a tendency to be flippant or insensitive with my words. One time I made a joke out of a hobby that my friend really enjoyed. I remember this moment because she had the courage to tell me that I had just hurt her feelings. I made her feel small because I took a cheap shot at something I did not understand. It is so difficult to find and build relationships with people who will call you out when you hurt them and allow you the opportunity to seek forgiveness. This is a treasure because in these painful moments we come face-to-face with the gospel. From the pain of it all, abundance and true freedom become realities and not just ideas. When I hurt my friend and must ask for and receive her forgiveness, not only do I eat and drink the truths and power of the gospel; but in my friend, in that cosmic moment of transcendence, I meet God.

This feels a little awkward because I know my friend, my husband, and my family members are actually very messy people, and I am in danger of placing my dearest relationships on a pedestal and idolizing them above God. So creating a binary is tidier. It helps me say, "Those people are not God, so I have to find God away from those people." But this is a false binary where I place relationship with God and relationship with people on opposite ends of my spiritual identity. But Scripture is not simply a list of solitary spiritual disciplines. It is the Story of a gospel of intimacy.

The Location of God

I love asking students "Where is God?" Because it allows them to whack at a grapefruit-sized Sunday school question. "God is everywhere," they respond (often with a little eye roll). "Right!" I respond with an enthusiastic gesture toward an imaginary gold star.

"So God is everywhere. Is he in this room?"

"Yes."

"Is he in this pen?"

"Um, I guess so. Yes."

"Where exactly is God in this pen?"

"I don't understand. Where *in the* pen?"

"Yes. We have established that God is everywhere. So he must be in this pen, and this table, and the chair I'm sitting on . . ."

It is true that God is omnipresent. No doubt about that. But it isn't a very helpful concept practically. Fortunately, God gave us some better answers.

In Scripture, God's "with-ness," his tabernacling, was creative and beautiful. A pillar of fire, a pillar of cloud, the Holy of Holies, the words of prophets and poets, a burning bush, and a still, small voice. Then the Incarnation wrapped God in flesh. Jesus of Nazareth walked among us. He had a body and a voice. He laughed, he wept, he challenged Thomas to a foot race (probably. Just a guess). He is Immanuel, God with us. He died a real death and came back to life with a real body, a body so real that even locked doors and solid walls were less real (Jn 20:19-26). Jesus' body had real scars and enjoyed a good fish breakfast on the beach with friends (Jn 20:27; 21:12-13). And Jesus is still alive. He is seated at the right hand of God the Father (Lk 22:69; Col 3:1).

Then came Pentecost.

Pentecost was a game-changer. The God who is everywhere and the risen, bodily Jesus said: "We (as in I) have one more location to occupy." The Holy Spirit came down and inhabited . . . not muffins, or coffee, or kittens, but his people.

Yep. People.

Not to question God or anything, but have you *met* people? They are the worst.

But since the triune God already had a pretty good grasp on the beauty of intimacy and indwelling and relationship, the Holy Spirit came to us and provided an internal union with Christ that tabernacles *in us*. Messy, beautiful us.

So where is God? Where do we look to find him? I know you were rooting for kittens, but it's people. We cannot know God without them. People are not God. People are not perfect like God. But in some mystery and genius of our all-knowing, all-loving Savior, people now live as the temples where we find and experience the presence of God in the Holy Spirit.

Does it surprise you that from birth and for the whole of your existence, you feel this insatiable pull toward intimacy, toward relationship, toward others? If God is located in his people through the indwelling of the Holy Spirit, and it is in intimate relationships where we learn who God is and experience his gospel, then he has blessed us through the gift of desire. Our desire for intimacy works like true north, always orienting our internal compass to go to where he is. We will never stop desiring intimacy because God will never stop desiring us to be within and transformed by his marvelous grace.

And yes, we will find God, but we will also find the mess. We have everything we need in the gospel to navigate this, but it is still hard. The effects of the fall still burn in us, and our shame breeds fear, lies, and sin.

But here is the good news. We are not doomed to be creatures of the fall, relentlessly gnawed to death by shame. Shame may be an enemy of intimacy, but intimacy is a tool of the Lord's to fight back against the curse. Through the gospel, intimacy becomes a deadly enemy of shame.

Where shame calls us to isolation, intimacy calls us to connection. Where shame tells us to hide, intimacy says, "Your vulnerability is wanted and made safe here." Where shame tells us lies, the gospel—being lived out in our intimate relationships—preaches truth to us, calling us back to the Light. "One of shame's most acute byproducts is the fear of exposure, the very thing that, paradoxically, is required for shame's healing," Curt Thompson reminds us.[1]

Shame and intimacy cannot coexist and flourish. Feeding one will always wilt the other. Shame has the power to make mountains out of molehills and tempt us to write manifestos in the dark. But if we lean into our intimate relationships, they will require us to connect, be vulnerable, be seen and known. And if they are living environments for the gospel, it will be the power of those relationships that allows Truth to cast out lies and Love to drive out fear. Those ghosts that haunted us in the dark are exposed in the light. They lose their power to influence and deceive. No wonder God gifted us intimacy through his triune nature to allow a way for all the doctrines, stories, and truths of the gospel to grow arms and legs and wrap themselves around us. Through intimate relationships, we get to see, experience, and be transformed by the presence and gospel of the Lord.

The Blessing of Solitude and the Ache of Loneliness

Wait a minute, that all sounds nice, but you can't tell me that I am unable to commune with God on my own. Even Jesus had to get away from people to go and be with his Father.

True. And because you are also a temple of the Holy Spirit, you have access to the Father. Before we go back to the necessity of relationship to engage the gospel, let's just take a moment to talk about solitude, isolation, and loneliness.

There is a whole world to explore of spiritual disciplines that include silence, meditation, and solitude. Learning how to be alone with the Lord is something every Christian must regularly practice. In fact, solitude enables us to have healthy, intimate relationships. Henri Nouwen wisely remarked, "Solidarity is the other side of intimacy."[2] This is true in two important ways.

First, if we cannot be alone or if we require people to be near us and with us at all times, this is an unhealthy trait often referred to as enmeshment. No relationship can endure constancy where the other persons become the object or the function of our needs. Sherry Turkle, in her study of online relationships and habits, notes that people are burying themselves deeper and deeper in artificial, virtual, or parasocial "relationships" because they are desperately seeking a feeling of connection. When we recognize our inability to have moments of solitude or silence, it exposes our sickness.

The second way solitude enhances intimacy is in the result of the practice. Both Richard Foster and Thomas Merton write about how solitude is successful if it increases love, empathy, and desire for others. Solitude is a key variable to any healthy relationship. But what we often fear or mistake for solitude is isolation and loneliness. These are what Turkle refers to as "failed solitude."[3] We need to discuss this because isolation is a tool of shame, and loneliness plays a major role in our own philosophies of relationship.

The Spiritual Wound We All Carry

I had my back turned to my friend, Collette. I was at her kitchen table finishing breakfast and she was behind me at the sink. "Loneliness is a force of nature," I remarked without turning around. We had been talking about my intimacy research and noting how things like loneliness are such a strong motivation for making unhealthy choices in our relationships. I made my observation but when I heard no response, I turned around and saw her bent over the sink, tears running down her face. I knew she was going through a particularly difficult season. Her best friend had passed away from an illness at the same time she had broken off a six-year romantic relationship. Just like that, the people she confided in and leaned on the most, were gone. Even with a full career, wonderful kids, and a loving family, she was buckling under the added weight of an acute loneliness.

I can relate. Loneliness has been a recurring theme for me the past few years. It has forced me to reckon with certain realities of my own life. It forces me to ask different questions: How does one cure loneliness? What do we do in moments when loneliness seems to steal the very oxygen from our lungs? Everyone I know has struggled with loneliness, and this struggle has not always been dictated by circumstances. There are plenty of us who have a discernable void of intimacy in our lives. This void, in its various manifestations, haunts us and triggers a sharp pang of loneliness.

But there are also those of us who are surrounded by loving people, healthy relationships, regular intimacy, *and yet* there is a loneliness we cannot shake. Over and over again, I witness people in a range of circumstances that suffer from loneliness. It leads me to agree with what scholars and poets have long observed: loneliness can plague any and all of us despite our circumstances. As a result, there seems to be no real fool-proof cure for loneliness. It cannot be eradicated by the perfect arrangement of intimate relationships sustained over long periods of time. Loneliness, it seems, must be about something much deeper.

This dilemma raises the question: If loneliness is not eradicated by the presence of healthy, sustained intimacy, then what is it that makes us lonely? What is this ache signaling? To put it simply, loneliness is not a physical but a spiritual condition. The ache lives in us all because no matter how good our relationships are with other people, they are never truly everything we need. People, even good people, are broken and flawed. No human relationship can fulfill all we crave and need. Additionally, even our current relationship with God does not eradicate the loneliness. While God is not broken or flawed, our relationship with God is. Even though God is with us in the most intimate way—the indwelling of the Holy Spirit—we still struggle with loneliness.

In an important and powerful way, the ache of loneliness is an ever-present reminder that the wholeness and connection we crave, the very fellowship we are created for, will not be fulfilled until all things are made new in the second coming of Christ. Until everything is fully redeemed and set right, the "already but not yet" leaves a mark of the rupture on our souls. We get foretastes of the kingdom in the beauty of our relationships with God and one another, yet these are still just shadows and signs pointing to the justice and restoration we all long for. Loneliness is a spiritual wound we carry with us. We can comfort each other in the solidarity of this condition. We can welcome the ache knowing it will not last forever and that Christ's redeeming work is moving even now, inviting us in.

Don't Ignore the Ache, but Don't Build on It Either

This leaves us with a new question: If loneliness cannot be eradicated or cured this side of heaven, what do we do with the deep pain of loneliness in our lives? Just because we all harbor this eschatological ache does not mean that loneliness isn't sometimes an unbearable weight. We must take loneliness seriously because it can be very dangerous.

I read a recent study on how loneliness can alter our brain's ability to discern threats.[4] I was stunned! We can be so crippled by loneliness that we become less able to make discerning choices about our safety. Loneliness is the number-one reason my students give as the motivation for seeking relationships. But if our fear of being alone is the guiding motivation, we are opening ourselves to all kinds of woes.

When loneliness is our motivation, we are tempted to reduce our relationships to functions. The accessible people in our lives act like a hit of morphine to symptoms of our struggle. If alleviating the pain of loneliness is consuming us, we will welcome even toxic and artificial forms of intimacy to replicate the effects of real intimacy and medicate our ache. And we will suffer double disappointment when what we thought would cure us only hurts us without ever ridding us of our ache.

Shame and loneliness feed off each other in powerful ways. Shame gets us alone and feeds us lies that our loneliness cosigns. So we take the options that technology provides, or we settle for unhealthy people in our dissolution and exhaustion. This fear of loneliness robs us of our true freedom. Keeping loneliness as our central motivation is like having a magnet too near our compass. It throws us off course. Henri Nouwen observed:

> How often is the intimate encounter of two persons an expression of their total freedom? Many people are driven into each other's arms in fear and trembling. They embrace each other in despair and loneliness. They cling to each other to prevent worse things from happening. Their sleep together is only an expression of their desire to escape the threatening world, to forget their deep frustration, to ease for a minute the unbearable tension of a demanding society, to experience some warmth, protection, and safety. Their privacy does not create a place where they both can grow in freedom and share their mutual discoveries, but a fragile shelter in a storming world.[5]

Steven sat in my office one day after the pain of a breakup. He realized that the relationship was not going anywhere but was sick with anxiety over the alternative that would leave him without a companion and back in a state of loneliness. Being very familiar with this state, he was already dreading the feelings, habits, and sins he often turned to. Without a companion, how was he to survive the symptoms of his loneliness?

Steven raises an important observation that many of us understand well. It doesn't help that we are swimming in a culture of romance idols. We are all fighting the saturated messages that relentlessly tell us our value and wholeness is found in having "someone." But even if the culture were not this way, our own longings indict us. We fear loneliness.

But I want to offer a slight shift: I do not believe it is loneliness we fear. What we actually fear are the things loneliness reveals. Sherry Turkle writes, "One might assume that what we want is a preponderance of weak ties, the informal networks that underpin online acquaintanceship. But if we pay attention to the real consequences of what we think we want, we may discover what we really want."[6]

This became a turning point in my own struggle with loneliness. For years, I experienced a crippling amount of loneliness. Not the on-again, off-again loneliness that is common to most of our lives—I found myself in a pit of real isolation where I could not name a person who truly saw me, knew me, and was curious about me. There were days I thought my ribs might fracture from the weight I felt. Yet in my search for some kind of hope, I was struck by the reality that, even if things began to change for me and this burden grew lighter, there were no circumstances or relationships that could ultimately eradicate my loneliness or banish it forever from my life. This meant that, because of this eschatological longing, my loneliness would always be with me even in some small way.

If this is true, then what are all my efforts for? What am I trying to accomplish? What is the point of these relationships if they cannot cure my loneliness? And if my loneliness is sharp and unbearable, am I just doomed to a life of pain management? What is my loneliness showing me about myself?

I suggested to Steven, and to you my brothers and sisters, that loneliness is not just a signpost to the anticipated consummation of Christ's work; it is also a signpost to the very brokenness that haunts our lives. In a way, loneliness is a doorway, and once we walk through it and cross its threshold, we discover that behind the initial panel of our loneliness are the actual issues we are suffering from. For Steven, it was not just loneliness but *who he was when he was alone* that brought shame and discomforting revelations. If loneliness was the diagnosis, then a relationship was the cure. If he stopped at the threshold and reasoned that all he needed was a companion, then he would be caught in an ongoing cycle of relationships in hopes that this circumstance would somehow fix the problem.

If loneliness is actually an invitation to peer into the dark, then when our eyes adjust, we find that there are other things driving the pain we describe as loneliness. And what is the advantage of finding these other things in our lives? It allows us clarity to see the intersections of our struggle and God's grace. We have the opportunity to surrender ourselves to the surgical work of sanctification. It relieves us from the mania of pain management so that we can learn what the Lord is doing in our life and step in as participants in that work. It takes us down new roads. Loneliness will always be with us, but we can finally learn to embrace this spiritual condition because we can know *why* it is in our life. And along this new road, we get to see deserts turned into gardens and beauty for ashes in other areas of our life.

A Kind of Grief

Another reframing that helped me confront my own struggle with loneliness was when I recognized that loneliness is a kind of grief, and any fresh grief can trigger the pain of the voids in our life. One friend recently described how, on her way to a funeral, the acuteness of her singleness suddenly rushed unexpectedly to the surface.

All our unmet longings, no matter how well we have managed them or come to peace with the circumstances in our lives, can be conduits of the spiritual condition of loneliness. Whenever grief or the deep brokenness of our world collides with us, an electric shock connects between seemingly unrelated parts of our story, and they become conductors creating a cross-section of voltage. This, too, is part of the economy of God. There are some wounds that do not heal in our lifetime. There are some longings that go unmet. This inaugurated kingdom of the "already and not yet" still contains cancer, violence, divorce, and death along with the powerful redemptive realities of healing, peace, intimacy, and life. The gospel compels us to hold all these truths with both hands.

Our loneliness is an evergreen tree in a forest of hardwoods that cycle continuously through seasons of abundance and bareness. If we can recognize and embrace this, then loneliness can be a valuable part of our life and not simply some malady we desperately need to cure. It loses its teeth when we realize that what we fear is not actually loneliness, but the darkness it reveals. And the good news comes when we remember that even darkness is not dark to God and night shines like the day (Ps 139:12). God, through Christ and the Holy Spirit, is invading our dark places with the restorative power of grace and love. Set in its proper place in the gospel, our loneliness is no longer a problem to solve but a sign to pay attention to. It is a guide to the indelible, sanctifying work of the Holy Spirit. And it releases our relationships from the untenable burden to fix something they can never fully repair.

A robust theology of intimacy invites us to the joy and the pain. It shows us the path and guides us with true north, but it does not ignore, nor does it revel in the ache. These work together, and only the gospel makes sense of their strange friendship. Being in relationships with other people is hard. They let us down. We let them down. We spend a lot of time and energy navigating the questions and assessing the circumstances in our dearest relationships. Are they mad at me? Why do I keep doing that? How do I get them to stop talking about themselves for the whole of our conversation? Why would he call me out like that? We spend endless hours deliberating over our choices and we hope to God that we are making good ones. We grope blindly because we have unmoored the economy of God in the gospel with the circumstances of our relationships and the condition of our hearts. But the gospel orients our brokenness and sanctification so that we can move forward asking better questions and relying on the truths the gospel has already provided.

I wish I could tell you that Collette's life and loneliness have turned around. I wish I could offer a miraculous turning point in my own ache and isolation. But for anyone journeying through these pages whose own heart is plagued by this same ache, I want to be honest: isolation and the weight of loneliness can be a very long, hard road, and I am with you in the solidarity of this struggle. I think my therapist would be proud of me for admitting this.

Not long after my visit with Collette, she decided it was time to find a local church. She had spent most of her life as an atheist, but in recent years, she drove miles to experience the urban megachurch where she first met Christ. But it had been a few years since she had physically been in church and this all came on a collision course with her grief. So she sought out a local church near her home with a fresh outlook for taking any flaws and mismatched preferences in stride, in exchange for the possibility of finding a worshipping community where she could begin to build intimate relationships with people proximate to her. Similarly, Mike and I moved halfway across the country, not necessarily for jobs as much it was for the prospect of finally being a part of a local church again.

I won't say that Collette or I have found a silver bullet to pierce the ache, but we do have hope. Time will tell, but I don't think it any coincidence that we both felt a pull toward church community. I'm keeping the door propped open on my own journey out of isolation, even if just a sliver. But a thin hope is still hope. And on this journey through a theology of intimacy, I am excited to show you what God has been showing me.

9

The Gospel Community of Remembrance

Formerly, when you did not know God, you were slaves to those who
by nature are not gods. But now that you know God—or rather are
known by God—how is it that you are turning back to those weak and
miserable forces? Do you wish to be enslaved by them all over again?

GALATIANS 4:8-9

You can't take the gospel seriously and not take your relationships seriously.

TIMOTHY S. LANE AND PAUL W. TRIPP

I imagine it is very hard work to have to head out of town and get all your
water from a well. I can only imagine that this task was made even more
difficult if you had to wait until the heat of the day.

There are clues as to why the Samaritan woman Jesus encountered
at the well had a broken life (Jn 4:4-26). Coming to get water at a time
when no one else came could be either because she was a social pariah,
or because she harbored shame, or perhaps she was not allowed out until
then. I don't imagine anyone would make this difficult chore even harder
on themselves if they felt they had a choice.

During their conversation, Jesus lets us in on some other details. This
woman previously had five husbands and the man she was currently with
was not her husband (Jn 4:17-18). Considering the very limited agency of
women in that time to have these kinds of options in their married lives,

we can safely assume that this was not something she desired or chose for herself. Marriage was more than a vehicle for sex and children in that era. It was economic safety and often the thin line between abject poverty and food on the table. Whatever injustices this woman had suffered, we can only imagine.

It always strikes me that Jesus chooses water and thirst as the gospel illustration to offer this woman (Jn 4:7-15). It makes a certain amount of sense because they are together at a well, but there is also something on-point for this woman specifically. It is as though thirst is the word that best describes her deep ache. She aches in a practical sense because of her especially difficult chore to draw the water at midday without other women. But it also speaks to the broken intimacy that haunts her life. We can detect evidence that all three spheres of her intimate life—friendship, marriage, and family—are broken. I hear my own plea emit through her as she asks Jesus to give her this Living Water so that she will never have to draw water or thirst again (Jn 4:15).

We just noted that loneliness can never be completely cured until the Lord returns and fully restores all things; this is why he is the Living Water. But in this world, we have an ongoing relationship with thirst. If I am thirsty, I can drink a glass of water and feel quenched for a few good hours. My thirst is at bay during this time, and I do not feel the sting of it. Like that glass of water, our intimate relationships can quell our loneliness. We need healthy, intimate relationships for many reasons, including that unchecked isolation, like dehydration, is dangerous. We are created for intimacy like our bodies are created for water. We cannot neglect our need for intimate relationships any more than we can stop drinking water every day.

But unlike the unreasonable burden to have people in our lives cure our loneliness, I have no delusions that a glass of water will keep me from thirst for the rest of my life or even the rest of the day. It would seem odd for me to quell my thirst with a glass of water to only, hours later, respond with indignance, "How can I possibly be thirsty again?!" Yet when the people in our lives do not eradicate our feelings of loneliness, we are dismayed.

If we can think of loneliness like we do water and thirst, we can enjoy the moments of reprieve that our healthy relationships bring us without superimposing unrealistic expectations on them.

I don't say this prescriptively as though eight glasses of water and twelve hugs a day are all we need to live lives that keep our physical and emotional thirst at bay. But if we go back to our ancestral first parents at the moment of their fall, we remember that we need something a bit stronger than hugs and hydration.

The Wealthy Homeless Man

One of the most damning effects of the fall is the deep-rooted deceit that lies in each of us. Shame fuels it, fear locates it, and our sin is a product of it. Like the first humans, our struggle begins with spiritual amnesia.

An old pastor of mine relayed this true story in a sermon one Sunday. A wealthy man in New York died, leaving his riches to his only living relative: his estranged brother. The deceased man's lawyers hired a private detective to track down his brother because it had been years since anyone had spoken to or seen him. It took nearly two months, but the detective finally found him in Utah. He was homeless, living on the streets, and sleeping in salvage yards.

It is not every day a homeless person inherits $100,000. The story made it into the newspapers.[1] The article reported how astonishing it was that this man, who had nothing, was transformed overnight into a man of means. And yet it wasn't overnight. On paper and legally, during those two months of searching, he had plenty of money. Yet this "wealthy" man woke up every morning on the streets, eating out of dumpsters and pushing a shopping cart with all his belongings.

My pastor asked, Why would a man with means eat lunch out of a dumpster? Simple. He did not yet know he was an heir. And when you do not know you have something, you live as though you don't have it.

It is like losing your keys and tearing the house apart only to discover they were in your pocket all along. The truth that you are in possession of your keys does not matter if you have forgotten. Not knowing you have something amounts to living like you don't have it.

Let's imagine it is now six months later. The homeless-man-made-prosperous has an apartment, a comfortable bed, and food in the refrigerator. Knowing this, we are dumbfounded when we turn a corner and find him digging for lunch in a dumpster. We would be perplexed. We might even say: "Friend, what is wrong? Don't you remember? You are a man of means. Go get lunch from a restaurant or make a club sandwich in your apartment. You do not need to get lunch from a dumpster. This is not your reality. This is not who you are."

My sisters and brothers, do you know who you are?

More than information, or doctrine, or theology, I have seen this question drive people to the gospel. In critical moments, Scripture shows Jesus combating sin and shame by anchoring people to their true identity. Indeed, even the woman at the well, who had quite the scandalous chat with Jesus, was not moved by his prophetic prowess or even the offer of Living Water. As she ran back through her village she exclaimed: "Come meet someone *who knows everything about me!*" (Jn 4:28-29 paraphrase).

After Jesus' resurrection, Peter experiences spiritual amnesia. We see this evidenced in his decision to go back to fishing. His deep shame in denying his Messiah and friend probably lead him to think, *I'm no good as an evangelist or disciple anymore. I should just go back to what I know.* And he does. But Jesus, in his brilliance and love, uses this to effectively re-create the very scenario, down to the details, of when he first called Peter to follow him (Lk 5:1-11; Jn 21:1-9). And even after an enthusiastic reunion and breakfast on the beach, we see Peter's shame shroud him. But Jesus knows that being seen, being known, being brought from isolation to combat the lies, is the way you conquer shame. It must have been devastating to Peter at first when Jesus asked, "Do you love me?" Peter could not bring himself to meet the standard of Jesus' question with his response. The sense memory of the charcoal fire and Jesus' three-peat question likely sent Peter into the painful recollection of his denial.

But after every time, Jesus responded with a reaffirmation of Peter's call. When Jesus repeated that Peter should feed his sheep, he was saying so much more. "Peter, you are not a fisherman. I called you to be a minister and a leader. Your betrayal does not disqualify you. I am telling you who you are. Remember who you are. Do not let your shame lie to you about who you are."

Being seen and known for who we are is crucial to both intimacy and the gospel.

But isn't all this identity jargon a secular narrative? Aren't we saturated with movies and celebrity culture that wants us all to believe in ourselves and "just be me"? Aren't identity politics just another thing dividing us?

Yes. The only way this focus on our identity leads to Christ is when it lives in the context of the gospel.

What Saints Require

When Christ was crucified and conquered death in resurrection, the kingdom was inaugurated, and it changed the world. But all of us, after finding Christ, still wake up to a broken reality, broken relationships, and a broken self. It may not feel or look like a changed world, but the New Testament tells us that the gift of the gospel of Christ is a new identity (Col 3:5-11). We are a new creation (2 Cor 5:17). As the intimacy motifs show us, we shift from isolation and slavery to freedom and adoption. We are children of abundance and not scarcity (Lk 11:3; Jn 6:48; Eph 1:23; Col 2:9-10). We are heirs of beauty and not ashes (Is 61:3). We have everything we need for life and godliness (2 Pet 1:3).

But how do we know that this is true? In this theology of intimacy, we meet a God who is not only loving, but relational, sovereign, near, cosmic, and intimate. Even so, this is also easy to forget. We are constantly fighting caricatures of God. But learning the identity of our triune God is critical for Christians. This is why the questions posed in Scripture that start with "How?" or "Why?" are often answered with "Who."

This is why we need to consistently come back to the Story. We need to worship, study Scripture, and pray. We need to come back again and again to these disciplines of remembrance. We must remember and engage the Story of God, so that we remember who God is, so that we remember who we are, so that we can live gospel-centric, flourishing lives. And yes, we need to do this as individuals, but I want to stress how important it is to practice these with others. *This is the most fundamental purpose of a theology of intimacy.*

We are hardwired at birth for and spend our whole lives seeking intimacy. We are driven by a thirst and ache because God wanted to make it difficult for us to isolate. We seek out intimacy because these are the very places where we learn who we are. We find our true identity by learning who God is as we engage the Story of God again and again.

Stanley Hauerwas got it right when he said, "Saints cannot exist without a community, as they require, like all of us, nurturance by a people who, while often unfaithful, preserve the habits necessary to learn the story of God."[2]

This is critical because we are drowning in an ocean of lies about who we are. In North American Western culture, sex, consumerism, relationship status, productivity, and success are leveraged to measure our worth and value. We sit in our churches and can feel the power differential between the married and unmarried. My students believe that academics, achievement, and marriage or an active sex life are what give them value. They may not say it out loud, but their anxieties and choices betray them. We are being dismembered by lies, and our spiritual amnesia is strong.

Even as a minister who preaches this gospel to my students every week, I find myself back at the dumpsters of my favorite sins. And it is not just my bad behaviors but my good behaviors that fuel my own functional atheism. Many days I believe that I am living in a world of scarcity—I am lonely and I shame myself for not being a better person. I am bitter at a God who seems to have left me to fend for myself. No one is going to champion my needs today, so it is all up to me. I will do whatever I need to feel whole and worthy. We are all being dismembered by these lies.

But we are called to remember.

The Spiritual Practice of Remembrance

Depending on your English translation of Scripture, the word *remember* is used around 165 times. One of the interesting facts of this word in Scripture is not just how often it is used, but where it is used. Outside of the Psalms, there are three main areas of Scripture where the word emerges: Deuteronomy, the prophets, and the New Testament epistles. As you comb through the places where remembrance is pronounced, a pattern emerges of people in transition.

In Deuteronomy, Moses gives his final state of the union before Israel enters the Promised Land. In the prophets, the people of God are in exile. And in the epistles, the Apostles work through the trials and joys of a diverse and growing church across the empire. When we remember, we are not just recalling something. To *re-member* is the antithesis of *dis-member*. When we remember we take something that used to be whole but was torn asunder, and reconstitute it: we re-member. This is what God does through his gospel. The biblical arc of creation, fall, redemption, and consummation tells this story: what was dismembered is being re-membered.

So Moses, after leading twelve tribes out of slavery and through the wilderness, commissions a people who are only just starting to think of themselves as a unified nation for the first time. He pleads with them to remember. To remember the mighty acts of Yahweh, because, by remembering those acts, they remember what kind of God they serve. And by remembering what kind of God they serve, they learn who they are.

Then the plea for remembrance is sparsely mentioned in the Story, until suddenly this once mighty nation of kings and God's chosen people is in exile. They need more than ever to remember who they are. They need to remember the Story of God, so that they can remember what kind of God called them to be his people, so that they can value their identity, even while strangers in a strange land surrounded by idols.

Then in the epistles, this brand-new thing, the church, is growing rapidly in its infancy. Facing racism, cultural divisions, classism, and sin, they are called over and over again to remember the Story of God. They are called to remember the Story so that they can remember who God is. They need to remember that God is a loving Father who sent his Son by taking on flesh and becoming one of us. To remember who this triune God is equips them to know and understand who they are. From this they can become communities of remembrance.

For you see, the idols that tempted our ancestors are no less potent today. And they do not call us with gross temptations we are prone to identify and repel, but by selling us a thousand small lies every day that cause us to forget who we are. Our most potent sins appear when we forget who we are in Christ.

Instead of remembering what the gospel says is true about you and me right now, without any qualifiers, that we are full and free, adopted and beloved—we forget.[3] Instead of fullness, we feel the sting of scarcity. We absorb lies that tell us that our hard work will be taken for granted, our saving accounts are not enough, our leaders are not enough, our efforts will not be enough to keep us full and whole—that we are not enough. Instead of remembering that we are free, we willingly reshackle ourselves and others to the golden fetters of expectations, disappointment, anger, exploitation, and small-mindedness. We question everyone's motives and build walls to protect ourselves because we do not remember that they also are beloved. And we do this because we do not remember that *we are beloved*.

When We Lose Who We Are

Once Bastian has saved Fantasia from The Nothing, he enters the Never-ending Story. He has many adventures but must find his way back using a magical amulet he wears around his neck. With it, he can make wishes that instantly come true. Like most of us I imagine, his first wishes are to make himself taller, stronger, and more handsome. As the story goes on, he becomes more selfish, greedy, and closed-minded, because with every wish he loses a memory.

After he has used his wishes to isolate himself, betray all his friends, and dash all his ambitions, he finds himself in a strange place where other children like him wander aimlessly. They push shopping carts filled with junk and wear shoes on their heads like hats. It is explained to Bastian that these are other child visitors to Fantasia who used their wishes unwisely. They used up all of their wishes, lost their memories, and forgot who they were before making it back to their world. The sight of this haunts Bastian and is a catalyst for his newfound urgency and wisdom in the rest of the story.[4]

Like Bastian, when we witness the fruits of spiritual amnesia in others, it is an opportunity to see it in ourselves. We live in the ruins of spiritual amnesia, wading through a sea of lies which undo our secure identities. The timeless sin of idolatry is only able to exist when we forget ourselves, because our idols are the symbols of our desperate need to place our hope for freedom and fullness in something.

Yet because of Christ, we do not need to strive for freedom or fullness; it has been accomplished for us. It is given as a free gift of grace by our Savior. The journey of sanctification is not earning or striving to attain our freedom and fullness. Sanctification is the process by which we learn more deeply who God is and who we are so we can live out of the identity that is *already ours*.

But how will we remember?

Having been a follower of Christ since I was a child, I am aware that a lifetime of listening to sermons, reading books, memorizing Scripture, being moved by worship music, and practicing daily devotions, sadly, does not ensure a regular, meaningful encounter with the gospel.

I still forget who I am. I ache with scarcity and want, even though my Savior has told me I am full. I feel incomplete, even though I am complete in the blood of Christ (Heb 10:14; 1 Jn 2:5). I don't feel free, even though this is what is already true about me because of Christ (Gal 5:1).

And this is why we need a robust theology of intimacy. We cannot do this on our own.

Not only do I need relationships, but I need my life to be woven together with intimate relationships whose fundamental purpose is the gospel. I need my friendships, my family, and my marriage to all be communities of remembrance. We must regularly gather to learn the Story of God so that we can know who God is, know who we are, and then live lives as the people we actually are.

Bastian finally makes it to the last gate that will take him back to his world and his father. The gatekeepers have only one question for him: "Who are you?" But Bastian used his final wish and memory to get to the gate and so he stands there with no recollection of his life or who he is. He cannot answer, and so he cannot continue.

It is a dreadful thing to lose ourselves. Because of the fall, we are in danger of the same deception that attempts to sell us a different identity. It is an identity based on fear and poverty, where we are led to believe that our circumstances and status get to own us and define us. It is a powerful deception that sells. What hope do we have to combat such a strong lie?

As if by some magic, Bastian's two friends, Atreyu and Falkor, suddenly appear with him at the gate. It has been many chapters since we have seen either of them. Bastian, in the process of losing himself, destroyed their friendship. But here they are. And upon hearing the unanswered question of the gatekeepers and seeing that Bastian had lost all memory, Atreyu answers the gatekeepers on Bastian's behalf:

> Atreyu looked at him, then took him by the hand and cried: "He's
>   Bastian Balthazar Bux!"
> The Gatekeepers: "Why doesn't he speak for himself?"
> "He can't," said Atreyu. "He has forgotten everything."
> "Without memory, he cannot come in."

Atreyu replied: "I have stored up everything he told us about
himself and his world. I vouch for him."

"By what right?"

"I am his friend," said Atreyu.[5]

If our intimate relationships are not built on being communities of
remembrance, then we have missed the point. Our friendships, family,
and marriages are all created to be the places where we live out and
learn the Story. They are where we locate God in the Holy Spirit. They
are where we store up the stories of each other's lives and become their
keepers. We do this so that when we see each other slip away from
who Christ says we are, like Atreyu, we become the ambassadors of
the gospel to each other. We get to be the ones who say, "You do not
need to eat out of that dumpster. This is not who you are. Come back
to who you are."

Jesus Christ stands before the Father and claims us. Our identity is
secure because we are the friend, the bride, and children of God. And just
as the Gatekeepers approved Atreyu's friendship as acceptable to allow
Bastian to cross the threshold, Christ's claim allows us communion with
the Father and entrance into his kingdom. We are bestowed the gift of
intimacy so that in our relationships we can reflect this scene again and
again. Because Christ is the friend whose blood covers us and allows us
entrance, we get to have and be the friends who stand in the gap of truth
and lies and remind each other who we are.

The Purpose of Intimacy

Back in chapter one I said that the highest aim of intimacy is a generative
closeness that refreshes and affirms one's identity and value, while simultaneously doing the same for the other person. This is the picture of that
aim, and it reframes our entire approach to relationships.

Why do you date? Why do you want to get married? What is the point
of friendship? Are you the kind of friend who reminds others who they
are? Why even try to have healthy relationships with my bipolar mother

or distant sibling? If we know what our relationships are ultimately for, we can begin to trace a line back to the questions we have about them and see them with new clarity. No longer can we claim a false binary that pulls us between "a relationship with God" and "a relationship with others." Within our relationships, a healthy practice of solitude and intimacy is the framework God set up so that we can know him. We will engage our relationship with him within our relationship with others. We cannot be the body of Christ or use our spiritual gifts without others.

But we can take our intimate relationships for granted. We can reduce the purpose of intimacy to superficial, functional, or selfish pursuits. But if we do, we are in danger of missing out on the engagement of the gospel, on being grace givers and grace receivers, on a process of sanctification, and on communities of remembrance. We are in danger of losing the tangible, vital avenue of gospel truth the Lord has gifted to us.

My sisters and brothers, when you and I remember who we are, when we realize we are full and free and that our Father has delighted to give us the kingdom, we live our lives with hearts on fire. When I come full and free to my work, my relationships, and my life, I come with the freedom to love others. I can do this because no lie of scarcity has made me believe that I need something from them to affirm my worth and value. I am already valued and loved. Now, I can just enjoy the people in my life.

Your circumstances will still be a mix of joy and pain. This world is broken and fraught with trouble. But hear this: these circumstances, while very real, no longer get to own you or define you. Christ has delivered the good news. We are a new creation, and our identity is found in him.

And even more good news, now we know where to find him. I barely considered that marriage, friendship, and family were not simply civic institutions conceived of by humankind. Our Lord created them from his own imagination so that he could communicate important and essential truths about who he is. He created them so that we could be in a living lab of gospel experience, where we are faced again and again with the truth of who God is and who we are. Then our relationships become a witness to these gospel truths. How we fight; how we spend money; how we forgive; how we relate to our sexuality, our past, and our whole lives now become a witness to this gospel. Our most intimate relationships become a city on a hill that draws the lonely, broken, and exhausted to the Light.

Part Three

WHERE WE GO
FROM HERE

Implications for the Local Church

*And since no man is an island, since we all depend on one another, I cannot
work out God's will in my own life unless I also consciously help other men
to work out His will in theirs. His will, then, is our sanctification, our
transformation in Christ, our deeper and fuller integration with other
men. And this integration results not in the absorption and disappearance
of our own personality, but in its affirmation and its perfection.*

THOMAS MERTON, *NO MAN IS AN ISLAND*

10

Examining Intimacy
in Our Gospel Communities

*Because we loved you so much, we were delighted to share
with you not only the gospel of God but our lives as well.*

1 Thessalonians 2:8

*Our love for one another must be rooted in a deep devotion
to Divine Providence, a devotion that abandons our own
limited plans into the hands of God and seeks only to enter
into the invisible work that builds His Kingdom.*

Thomas Merton

My friend Mallory is single and loves her church. She told me a story about something that happened to her one Sunday morning.

She had arrived shortly after the start of the service. She walked past the welcome table where an older couple was handing out name tags. She quickly and quietly took a seat in a row by herself, because it is not uncommon for her to be seated by herself. This was not indicative of her relationship to her church. The clergy know her well, and she had been very involved in small groups, book clubs, service outings, and various committees for a few years. But since she is single, one of her least favorite Sunday morning practices is when everyone stands and greets each other; she would usually do this quickly and sit back down. But on this particular morning, the older gentleman from the welcome table came up to where she sat.

"Are you all on your own?" he asked her. But without waiting for a reply, he followed this with the exclamation, "Well, that won't do!"

Mallory waited to hear the result of his observation. Would he invite her to sit with him and his wife? Would he ask her about herself? Would he sit with her?

Nope.

He just turned and walked away. That was it.

As Mallory relayed this story, we laughed because it could easily be a parody of how single adults experience the church. That older gentleman may not know it, but he accurately executed a well-worn script known to many a single adult in churches. For them, too often being at church offers a repeating cycle of (1) shedding light on their being alone, (2) asserting that this is not how it should be, and then (3) doing nothing helpful.

After looking at a robust theology of intimacy, we can't neglect its implications. This is not a simple application as much as it is embracing something already at work on us and in us. Our intimate relationships, vertical and horizontal, have a symbiotic relationship with each other. Our relationship with God and others is woven together in more profound ways than we may have known. This theology of intimacy is more than a set of beliefs; it is a gospel reality that reframes the day-to-day engagement of our intimate relationships. Because of the Christian anthropology of a theology of intimacy, we need to shed light on how this will have an impact on people's lives and, largely, the church politic.

Emerging Adults and the Church

I am a deacon in the Anglican Church of North America, and I get to serve at a local church parish alongside two Anglican priests. I am also a chaplain at a large Christian university. My life is always suspended between the local church and the culture of emerging adults. There is no escaping the relevance of pressure points between Christian emerging adults and the local church. A significant implication for the local church is connected to how we care for and communicate with this demographic.

Eighteen-to-twenty-eight-year-olds are certainly not the only demographic in the local church, and are not any more or less important than any one represented there. But a robust theology of intimacy is especially meaningful to this group and their relationship to the local church.

First, this is a group asserting agency, often for the first time, on whether they will attend church and how they will choose it. Second, this group is categorically crossing thresholds of significant intimate relationships. Scholars often refer to time between eighteen and twenty-eight as "the defining decade."[1] More than any stretch of ten years, emerging adults make decisions that will significantly affect their adult life. Leaving home, higher education, vocational discernment, buying homes and cars, moving to new cities, and navigating marriage and possibly children are all hallmarks of this life stage. The value and involvement of a local church has an immense impact on individuals emerging into adulthood. If you are a minister like me, I would strongly urge you to think through the need for a robust theology of intimacy. Emerging adults are choosing churches in a tumult of relationships. Whether they are aware of this or not, the implications of a theology of intimacy carry weight. For Mallory, there is a tension between loving her church and wondering if it is truly a place for her.

In chapter three I shed light on the sad reality that our anemic theology of intimacy produces the affirmation of hierarchies based on relational status. I saw this reflected in a conversation I had recently with a man who has two churches. On Sunday mornings, he attends a local church with his family but attends another church alone on Sunday evenings. Even though he is married with kids, attending church alone heightens feelings of inferiority that single persons often feel. No one has said anything explicitly, nor has he been treated poorly in any way. But with so many young families and other households in the small evening congregation, he struggles with this invisible stigma. This is how pervasive and quiet these artificial hierarchies are. As one of my friends described, it's like glitter. You must work really hard to remove it and it seems to just show up randomly. Unless we combat this intentionally as leaders of our churches, it will quietly but deliberately ascribe value and worth to our people based on their relationship status.

Additionally, in his book *From Isolation to Community*, Myles Werntz draws attention to how the internal structure of most Western churches is ordered via individuals (or even individual households) instead of a community. The cultural pull of autonomy, entitlement, and productivity seeps into our latent ecclesiology. As a result, the local church in North American Western culture is always in danger of allowing church to function as individuals practicing spiritual liturgies in crowded rooms. "Ultimately, if what the church is can be performed by the individual without remainder, then we gather not because anything is materially altered in us when we gather but because we wish to not be doing these alone."[2] Our inattention to this as leaders will reinforce these patterns of consumerism and autonomy. A corporate gathering does not automatically ensure a living body of Christ. For emerging adults, whether married, unmarried, children, no children, divorced, sexually active, or celibate, there is a drive to discern how the struggle of their lives is seen and cared for by the local church.

Our solutions should not simply be programs or outreach. This is not a commercial for seeker-sensitive, nuanced evangelism. Like my friend Mallory, many emerging adults are not just looking for a place to be seen, but a place to serve. Their relationship status, however, will have a bearing on the way the church responds to both desires. Henri Nouwen articulates the struggle of my single friends when he observes:

Probably no word better summarizes the suffering of our time than the word "homeless." It reveals one of our deepest and most painful conditions, the condition of not having a sense of belonging, of not having a place where we can feel safe, cared for, protected, and loved.[3]

I am not saying that church should look more like a social club, nor am I prescribing ways for churches to simply be spaces where individuals can come, worship, and leave. Werntz reminds us:

> Describing the church involves two inextricable claims: (1) Christianity cannot not be social—that is, there is no such thing as a non-social life in Christ. And (2) Christianity is not merely social—that is, the church is not only a social institution but a gathered body within creation that is the body of the risen Son of God. There is no disentangled origin to being social and being in Christ, for the two come into view together.[4]

Our grasp of a robust theology of intimacy and our ability to live it out in the local church will provide the stabilizing bar needed to understand and attempt this critical balance. To this end, I invite us to examine all three spheres of intimacy as they appear in the lives of Christians. This is an introduction to first steps by breaking down implicit and explicit messages and motives in our theology of intimacy. Let's begin with marriage.

Marriage: Just the Two of Us (and God Sometimes)

As a minister to emerging adults, you can probably guess how big the topic of marriage is. Additionally, I see many churches taking this subject seriously with regular marriage seminars, sermon series, and programs focused specifically on engaged couples, newlyweds, and seasoned veterans of marriage. These and others are all good things, and I do not wish to disparage any of them. The problem is not when we take marriage seriously in our local churches; it is when we take it for granted or elevate it in dangerous ways.

Many churches have an overemphasis, even obsession with marriage (as the institution or the mechanism for sex and children). But this obsession often takes its cues from secular culture which leads us to the same dead ends. We have been negligent in how our programs, discipleship, and general approach to relationships is simply painting with the same colors but adding a Christian veneer. But we can make course corrections that will not only clean out the distortions seeping in from the outside but will allow us to recapture and re-center the gospel.

Like popular culture, we have adopted an anthropocentric approach to marriage. Terrell Owens's "I love me some me" is a kind of anthem for popular culture, but we have our own version in Christendom by using our personal fulfillment as a guiding standard for our relationships. Many of us learned as early as our dating days that we are looking for a person who will work to recognize and fulfill our needs (and that we are to do that for them).

But the brokenness of our lives complicates this well-meaning reciprocity as we struggle to think covenantally and not contractually about our marriages. As the years go on, we don't know what to do when we fail each other again and again. As clergy, we try to help these couples by explaining the balance of roles and the need for mutual servanthood. Best practices, sadly, are not enough for most of us to either keep our marriages together or see them flourish if we remain committed, but the rubric we use to measure is often the only one we know—*how this is affecting me*. Thomas Merton was right when he exclaimed, "To consider persons and events and situations only in the light of their effect upon myself is to live on the doorstep of hell."[5]

But what else is there? Marriage requires sacrifices and compromise. It also needs a sober assessment of mutuality and reciprocity. No one should be a doormat or martyr in their marriage. But without a firm grounding in the gospel, we are in danger of swinging between extremes in efforts to counter the conflict, sin, and isolation we encounter.

The poor frameworks of an autonomous, productivity-driven, entitled culture seep in when we lack a robust theology of intimacy to take its place. As a result, we often find ourselves using our personal fulfillment as a threshold for assessing our marriage. We reduce our partners and ourselves to commodities as we evaluate a tit-for-tat assessment of our situations.

When I was engaged to be married, I found myself at the kitchen table of a couple whose house I was staying at while traveling for work. Though they were referred through a mutual friend as a place to stay, I did not know until I stayed with them that they were marriage counselors. In the evenings I would sit with them, and we would have long, thoughtful conversations together. Dave, the husband, asked about my engagement and why I wanted to marry Mike. I responded with our story and how we had figured out what a good fit we were for each other and had fallen in love. I was sure to highlight all the benchmarks of our friendship and compatibility to really sell it. My host nodded politely and then asked, "Erin, what is the purpose of marriage?"

I had never really thought about it before, but I was able to piece together an answer that landed me on the gospel. I said that I figure marriage is, like the Bible says, a picture of the Lord and his bride. Somehow, our marriages are about the gospel and their purpose is to be a witness to others about that gospel. Dave grinned and asked again, "So, tell me, why do you want to marry Mike?"

My head kind of exploded.

For the first time, I realized that behind the fit, attraction, compatibility, commitment, and love was a choice and a call. I wanted to marry Mike because I believed that in and through our partnership in marriage we could be on mission for the kingdom and the Lord's redemptive purposes in the world even better together than we could apart. I believed that our marriage contained important aspects that would allow us the opportunity to shine a light on, with, and for the gospel. And this reframed everything.

If we look back on a theology of marriage in chapter seven, we see that marriage is both a spiritual and physical reality. The triune God uses this intimacy motif to communicate who God is. As Bridegroom/Lover/Spouse, we are forced to reckon with a God whose nature is fidelity and love. This God chooses us and draws us near. This mystical marriage is the wedding feast of the Lamb (Rev 19:7-9). As an act of reconciling us to himself, we are brought out of a life of scarcity and fear and into abundance and safety. Our salvation is marked by a closeness where God abides with us and in us. Marriage is a unique institution that is designed to capture the intimate nature of this spiritual invitation, and all of this is made possible by the ultimate act of self-giving love. The gifting love of marriage is the gifting love that comes from the cross. And it appears every time we confess, take responsibility, repent, repair, ask for forgiveness, and offer/receive forgiveness.

Just as the mysteries of our salvation are opened for us in the motif of marriage, we move beyond symbols as we see the gospel grow legs in our own marriages. If the purpose of marriage is to embody the living truths of the gospel, our aims and objectives are guided by this true north. It starts with the husband and wife who are, essentially, each other's front line of defense against shame and a false sense of self. Married couples get to achieve a unique level of vulnerability that allows them to, with confidence and consistency, preach the gospel to each other.

Like Atreyu, we get to look at one another and say: "This is who you are. Don't forget. Because of Christ you are adopted and loved. You are free and full. You are beloved, lacking nothing for life and godliness." We must be gospel reflections to each other. Because of our proximity and intimacy, our spouse is usually the first to see the signs of spiritual amnesia through sin, deceit, fear, and shame. Married partners occupy a special place of being gospel champions for each other first and foremost.

Do we preach the gospel to each other explicitly? Yes! But we also back it up in all the ways we live our life together. These gospel truths and our identity in Christ will and must affect all corners of our married life. It will change how we spend our money. It will frame how we parent. It will orient how we deal with conflict, sin, and failure. It will change how we approach sex.

Matt O'Reilly captures this when he writes:

> The question that must be asked is this: To what sort of god does our sexuality point? A self-oriented god? A god who breaks his promise? A god with whom we cannot be safe? Or does our sexuality point to a God who always keeps his promises, no matter how hard and no matter what is required? Does it point to a God who gives himself in love to a true other who is clearly distinct? Do our sexual practices point the world to a God who can always be trusted with our vulnerabilities? What does the way we use our sexuality say about the God we serve?[6]

With congruence in both our private and public life, and an anchoring in the gospel, our marriages become a city on a hill drawing everyone to Christ with their warmth and light.

I love this observation from Wendell Berry because it paints a picture of the marriage that is oriented on the gospel:

> Lovers must not, like usurers, live for themselves alone. They must finally turn from their gaze at one another back toward the community. If they had only themselves to consider, lovers would not need to marry, but they must think of others and of other things. They say their vows to the community as much as to one another, and the community gathers around them to hear and to wish them well, on their behalf and on its own. It gathers around them because it understands how necessary, how joyful, and how fearful this joining is. These lovers, pledging themselves to one another "until death," are giving themselves away, and they are joined by this as no law or contract could ever join them. Lovers, then, "die" into their union with one another as a soul "dies" into its union

with God. And so here, at the very heart of community life, we find not something to sell as in the public market but this momentous giving. If the community cannot protect this giving, it can protect nothing—and our time is proving that this is so.[7]

A world aching for beauty and restoration cannot help but be drawn by a household that fights well, forgives well, and is overflowing with generosity, humility, hospitality, and justice. A gospel-centered marriage does not dismiss the needs of the individual; it simply orients them in light of the Story. We remember that we are broken people who will continually fail, but are gifted with the very tools for repentance, repair, restoration, and sanctification. Marriage, like all intimate relationships, is a master class in forgiveness.

When our marriages really struggle and buckle under the weight of sin and shame, it does not matter how equitably we divided the chores or managed expectations. We will need rescue by a power that can bring back the dead. For many of us, our marriages have faced times where we cling to the gospel like that one plank that is left of our shipwrecked life. Yes, we may need to set hard boundaries, get counseling, and walk a slow and painful road, but it is the gospel of Christ that puts the tools in our bag. And it is the indwelling of the Holy Spirit that gives us the transcendent power to use them well.

Marriage is an important and unique intimate relationship that we must take seriously and shepherd well in our churches. We need good programs and sermons to ground couples in the gospel. But we must also dislodge marriage from the romance idolatry that has artificially elevated it above all other kinds of intimacy. Just as popular culture has made sexual attraction and activity the currency by which we place value on individuals, Christendom has taken the same concept and simply adapted it to marriage in an effort to sustain a traditional sexual ethic. But to do so without the orientation of the gospel is to simply change the color of the currency. The cultural milieu may ascribe value by your sexual attraction and activity, but in the church we value you based on how successful you are at landing a marriage partner.

The way we approach non-married people in our pews is the result of our romance idolatry and overemphasized view of marriage. We cannot take for granted how this hierarchy of relationship status permeates our church life and discipleship models. We place marriage as the ultimate achievement of Christian adults and can then only care for singles as those whose "season" is temporary. We may genuinely want people to not be lonely, but romance idolatry taints these well-meaning efforts so that they keep reinforcing a message about someone's personal value and worth.

And this damages marriage as well. There is a perceived pressure to "succeed" at marriage. Whether this is a flawless sex life promised after a commitment to celibacy, or the expectation to have children, or the Norman Rockwell Instagram life, an overinflated importance of marriage affects everyone. One tragic side-effect of marriage idolatry is how it isolates a couple. If getting married is considered a hallmark of our spiritual acumen, then there is an underlying idea that all we need is each other. To single out the marriage motif as God's favorite is to limit marriage to a microcosm of Christian success. Everything we need is right here, just the two of us.

But this is not the case.

Family: Everyone's Origin Story

I asked my favorite marriage counselor what he wished Christian couples knew as they approached marriage. Mike did not take long to say just how important the family of origin is in the health of our marriages. He brought to mind a story from a married couple, Andy and Jenny, who had come back from the brink of divorce. They spent several weeks at a marriage intensive for couples whose relationships were moving toward the exit. Andy and Jenny were surprised that instead of discussing their marriage, the counselors wanted to spend the sessions on how they grew up and their family dynamics during their formative years. It seemed strange at first, but they soon realized that everything toxic in their marriage had an origin story.

When we looked at the origins of our desire for intimacy as well as shame, we observed that our first scripts were written in our families of origin. Because of our love for autonomy, we are easily deceived into thinking that we simply popped from the head of Zeus, masters of our decisions and destiny. Our culture loves a good "Invictus" where "I am the master of my fate: I am the captain of my soul."[8] But the product of our adulthood has been forged in the lab of our upbringing. This does not mean that we are doomed or fated by our past. Family Systems Theory is a tool used by professionals to help married couples and individuals in counseling.[9] These tools, along with modern neuroscience, can now prove what the gospel has known all along: the rescripting of our attachment styles and neural pathways because of neuroplasticity enables us to "be transformed by the renewing of your mind" (Rom 12:2). But this transformation requires help and relationships.

So while our family of origin is significant to our adult relationships, family is also an ongoing intimate relationship that requires our attention. We all need a robust theology of intimacy for the family for two key reasons.

First, married couples who plan to have children would do well to consider the importance of the family as a significant intimate relationship. Just as marriage is a gospel motif to communicate God's identity and mission in restoring, gifting, and abiding, family is used significantly in Scripture for the same purposes. When we discuss whether or not to grow our families, are we thinking about the purpose of family as it is given to us through the gospel? I would love for everyone considering children to have a moment like I did with Dave as I was preparing for marriage. Why do we want children? Do our reasons center on the gospel and how a family embodies this truth? Just as our marriages are about more than individual fulfillment, families share a mission and purpose to be a light of the gospel.

We start here as we consider having children, but as our families grow, there is an additional caution. Romance idolatry has a friend, and her name is the idolatry of the nuclear family. I have pastor friends who lament the endless justifications of how travel-team baseball and theatre rehearsals are given more importance than church. Parents are busy with the active, well-rounded, extracurricular achievements of their kids. And why not? We want good things for our kids. We want them to have these activities and experiences to have a broadly developed upbringing, be able to get into good schools, become educated enough for well-paying jobs, start families, and live comfortably so that they can start the cycle over again.

But if the family has been designed by God to be an ecosystem of gospel life, then how we raise children, spend money, prioritize time, and build our lives will be reoriented to answer questions like this: How does our family preach and embody the gospel toward each other? How are we practicing the gospel in how we fight, forgive, serve, and learn? When we choose where to live, our schools, and our communities, are we thinking about how to leverage our gospel purpose of restoring, gifting, and abiding so that these spaces and people will know the Lord by being proximate to us and our household? It is not about getting families to prioritize youth group over basketball practice. Are we shepherding our congregations to know the gospel purpose of family in the lives they are building?

This works both forward and backward; the families we come from and the families we are creating with our lives. If emerging adults pursue futures of marriage and family, these considerations need to be calibrated by a theology of intimacy that reckons with why and for what purpose these institutions were created. We look forward to our emerging family, but also back to the family that formed us.

The second significant concept in our theology of intimacy in the family has to do with adult relationships with family. My emerging adults, like Brian, come into my office all the time to discuss the growing pains of transitioning from childhood to adulthood in relationship with their parents and/or siblings. With all the Christian books we have on dating, marriage, and sex, it is disheartening to discover the grievous lack of material about how to navigate this life stage with one's family of origin. It is a pervasive issue for my emerging adults, but the effects last long into adulthood.

For married couples, these adult relationships with family can contain pain points. It is impossible to get away from how those families impacted our development as a human, but it is also difficult to escape the effects of those relationships, even if absent, on our adult lives. Demographic statistics show that even with the transience of emerging adults, more than half eventually settle down somewhere close to either where they grew up or to their families of origin.[10] As complicated as families are, there is a glaring vulnerability in our need for family. Practically speaking, families usually come with the infrastructure for vital support systems in our adult life.

Single adults often see the benefit of having family close to help them if they are sick, stuck somewhere with a busted vehicle, in financial trouble, or in a housing transition. Married couples with children live in the tension of both benefits and liabilities in living close to their families. Having reliable emergency help with the unpredictability of young children can be a lifesaver. But if the relationships are unhealthy, it can be a risk traded tenuously for this benefit. It is difficult to replace the value of having family help when we find ourselves struggling. But without a gospel identity for family, these relationships often stay in a cycle of tension and bargaining.

While ministers might vent their frustration over the demotion of church life to the idol of the nuclear family, we can only look to the log in our own eye. The idol of the nuclear family begins with romance idolatry. As church leaders we, intentionally or unintentionally, place our people in a hierarchy. The industry of Christian books and resources on sex, dating, and marriage are byproducts of a consumer model in churches that invest in the cycle of dating/courting, engagement, marriage, and children for their congregants. Though I am a major proponent of churches being bastions for healthy relationships, romance/nuclear family idols sell us an anemic version that cheapens both marriage and family by commodifying them.

These idolatries are fueled by the autonomy and celebrated self-reliance of our North American Western culture. Popular media is littered with messages where the heroic couple must face down the tide of opposing voices: "Us against the world! Just you and me, babe." Similarly, but less often, we hear a family mantra that "All we need is each other. Family first." While these notions are romantic, they are not true. In fact, they are cleverly packaged lies.

When we do premarital counseling for couples, one thing we point out is the three-fold nature of a marriage. If you think of this as a pie chart, one part of the marriage is romance and sex. Often the romance and sex is a smaller sliver of time that gets even more difficult to fit in as we get older. But even though it is smaller, it is a very important piece. We should still work to keep the romance fun and consistent and to make sure the sex is mutual and deeply loving. But so much of life is actually taken up by the other two variables.

Another piece of the pie is the very not-sexy part of sharing a household. Marriages come with the need to function like any healthy roommate scenario. There is a constant negotiation of who will pick up groceries, drop off the kids, call the plumber, and take the dog to the vet. These are life things. We all have them. Healthy marriages can tackle these with the same respect and consideration that longstanding roommates do. It is not sexy or intimate, but there are toxic and healthy ways to navigate these essential components of any lived-in relationship. But don't let this take up too big a piece of the pie. It is very easy for marriages to slide away from intimacies into being glorified roommates.

The third piece is the biggest and most overlooked: the friendship. In a marriage, there is a lot that lies in between sex and chores. The healthiest marriages are able to recognize and cultivate the art of friendship. First and foremost, this friendship exists between the two individuals who are married, but the next concentric circle is a group of friends who have access to the marriage and help keep it healthy. In fact, neither marriages nor families are designed to live in isolation as solitary households. It isn't "us against the world." No single individual can be all the things we need. And even large families can develop toxic systems that need to be seen and corrected with outside help. If we believe that we have all we need in only a spouse or family, we have under-realized the gospel and the importance of friendship.

Friendship: The Foundational Intimacy

Friendship has been relegated to a supporting role for so long we have to fight to claim it as an intimate relationship. Our culture loves friendship, but often only as a step toward the main event: romance and sex. As Christendom has adopted these same patterns, we have neglected the art of friendship as a component of the gospel through the example of Christ.

A theology of intimacy highlights the composition of restoring, gifting, and abiding in how Jesus uses the motif of friendship in Scripture. We will need to abandon the cultural narrative about friendship and look to Christ to discover its importance. Wes Hill writes: "The good news of God in Christ took friendships based on preference and a pursuit of social status and made them about self-giving love. It took fellow citizens, acquaintances in the great societal circle, and made them brothers and sisters. After Christ, friendship would never be the same."[11]

And how would it never be the same? First, to claim friendship as an intimate relationship is a radical counterweight against hypersexualization. Friendship allows a space for intimacy without sex. It allows people to be more than just their sexual allure, objectification, and possession. Intimacy in friendship suddenly allows accessibility for a much larger group of people. Friendship is ageless and available to people of every stage of life. If we rediscover a deep and fulfilling intimacy in friendship, we can dislodge romance idolatry and resist the temptation to sexually commodify people. Additionally, if we can have friendships that provide and protect a beautiful intimacy where we are seen and known and cared for mutually, we can provide the picture of a celibate life that is not doomed to loneliness. No longer is the attainment of sexual or romantic intimacy the last word on being a full and fulfilled human being. *We are created for intimacy, whether we have sex or not.* Friendship allows this to be true.

Second, friendship is where all of us discover a different intimacy with God. To have friendship with God is the picture of the art of friendship. Christ communicates with us, making God's self known to us, and gives of himself in sacrificial love. In friendship with Christ, we learn the art of friendship and we learn who we are. Our identity is, once again, marked by the restorative and redeeming presence of intimacy. Christ's use of friendship not only gives us access to true freedom and intimacy, but it shows us that this is how we are created and who we are because of who Christ is. "Paradoxically, human freedom consists in the service of God, but of a God who does not call us 'servants' but 'friends.'"[12] Do we ever use our pastoral care appointments or our pulpits to help our people see this profound truth? We should.

Because the third way Christ changes friendship forever is in how it is tied to our very identity as the church. Friendship—not romance, marriage, or the nuclear family—is the hub of the intimacy motifs that secures and elevates all three of them. If we learn the art of friendship, our dating life, our marriages, and our families will improve. If in dating we learn the art of friendship, it will carry into our marriages. Emerging adults need the art of friendship to aid their transition from a child to having some kind of adult relationship with their siblings and parents. Additionally, both marriages and families need people outside of the immediate household who come around them and provide relational scaffolding for the health of their daily household life. And finally, friendship itself allows for *everyone* to have intimacy, despite their relationship status.

But for this to be true, we have to recognize the importance of friendship and why it is so central. Friendship is not central because of its accessibility alone. It is central because Christ placed it at the heart of our identity as the church.

11

The Art of Friendship
and the Family of God

God sets the lonely in families.

PSALM 68:6

What statement about friendship can be more sublime, more true,
more valuable than this: it has been proved that friendship must
begin in Christ, continue with Christ, and be perfected by Christ.

SAINT AELRED

As I was studying these three intimacy motifs in Scripture, I found myself captivated by the passage in John where Jesus talks to his disciples about friendship (Jn 15:13-15). It felt like a culminating moment for the intimacy motifs. I had already seen the momentum built on familial language and the spousal motif. Scripture has no lack of these. Their use is pervasive. But in the Gospel of John, Jesus says some astounding things about friendship that are stark and unwavering in comparison to how the other two motifs are handled in Scripture. To say that the self-giving, sacrificial love between friends is the greatest of all love is truly a mic-drop moment. You don't have to exegete deeply to see that Jesus thinks very highly of friendship.

Eager to unearth more on this motif, I scoured the Scriptures. But I was puzzled to discover what seems to be a considerable dearth of the motif of friendship in comparison to the other two. How can it be hailed with such importance by Jesus and then left silent in so much of Scripture?

As it turns out, though, I was wrong. Scripture is not silent on friendship. In fact, Scripture has a great deal to say about friendship. I just failed to see it at first.

I am deeply indebted to scholars like Wes Hill who revealed a catalyst for understanding the role of the friendship motif in the gospel and our lives. In the three synoptic Gospels a story is told that, at first, seems innocuous for our theology of intimacy. Jesus is preaching to a packed house. His mother and brothers arrive but can't get in to see him for all the people. Jesus gets a message that his mother and brothers are here, and in that moment, Jesus does one of his classic responses that starts with a cringe and ends with timeless wisdom. He says, "Who are my mother and brothers?" Then pointing to his disciples and followers he says, "Here are my mother and brothers. Anyone who will follow me is my mother and brother and sister" (Mt 12:46-50; Mk 3:31-35; Lk 8:19-21, author's paraphrase).

First, the cringe. It feels a little icky for Jesus to land what appears to be a diss on his bio-fam. But Jesus was not being dismissive or objectionable to his blood family. If we remember that God is the triune God, then Jesus is the Son of the same Father who gave the commandment to "Honor your father and your mother" (Ex 20:12). Yet Jesus also states that you have to leave or even hate your father and mother (Mt 10:35-37; Mk 10:29-30; Lk 14:26). But these seeming contradictions can be reconciled in this profound moment in the packed house. Wes Hill says:

> When Jesus is asked about his understanding of kinship and familial ties, he doesn't reject them as so much detritus from the old regime that his kingdom is displacing. Instead, he takes the basic notion of "family" and cracks it open, stretches its contents beyond their agreed-upon limits, and wraps the result around a much wider range of people than was socially acceptable.[1]

When Jesus calls his disciples his family, he orients the identity of friendship into the context of a family. Those same disciples he named as friends in John 15 are designated as family. We can say that biblical friendship is framed as family, and Scripture has a lot to say about family. When Jesus ties these two motifs together, it is groundbreaking for how we understand our relationships to one another. And indeed, this is how the church came to know itself from that moment on.

Born Again but into the Family of God

If you have ever been baptized or studied its significance in Christianity, you will know that the use of water is traced to many biblical symbols and stories. Water has been used throughout Scripture to show a passage of transformation. Baptism is a sacrament of death to life, new birth, and entrance into the living body of Christ in his church. And while we do not diminish the rich and varied significance in baptism, it is and has historically been a revelation of what Jesus proclaimed in that packed house. Indeed, if you see pictures of some of the earliest baptismal fonts from Christian history, their shape is undeniably anatomical. The not-subtle artistic renderings of a womb (and other such female parts) are clearly used in the design of the fonts. We need not wonder if the early church took seriously the significance of baptism as a new birth.

But new birth into what? Baptism is a public sacrament that involves and requires the activity of the local church. This is because the newly baptized are being welcomed into their new family, their chosen family. In the long course of history, we have reduced this concept to fading symbols and sentimental articulations. We might call each other brother or sister so-and-so. You may have priests or other clergy who are called father or mother. Similarly, outside the church, there are collectivist cultures that use a shorthand to refer to all elderly women as "auntie." We sing about the family of God, and we refer to the Eucharistic sacrament as Communion. But do we take it seriously? Is this family just a spiritual idea that has no lived significance? A theology of intimacy pushes back.

In our baptismal identity, we accept the framework of chosen family as the identity of the church. And this identity is not a mere symbol. We believe that Christ's death and resurrection provide us a gift of righteousness that we can access because of grace and the indwelling of the Holy Spirit. And while this new identity is given freely and abundantly, our ability to live out of that identity comes through a process of sanctification. We learn, we trust, and we remember, so that over time we are shaped by the working of Christ in us to better know ourselves as beloved, adopted, friends of God.

But this identity formation does not take place in a vacuum or the singular routine of individual devotional practice. "Identity formation must include not only various forms of refusal but also an active engagement in an alternative culture—a 'community of truth'—that forms them to see themselves and the world in a uniquely Christian way," notes Wendell Berry.[2] We need each other to do this. But it is not simply programs relayed through an institution. In fact, Scripture does not describe the church this way as all. Yes, we are a house, but we are "living stones" of a "spiritual house" (Eph 2:19-22; 1 Pet 2:5). We are a body, a vine, a household, a family. The language used to describe the church is organic, alive, and dynamic.

It is in this unique framework called the local church that we can actually experience the life-changing sanctification of the gospel. And this cannot be realized if we dislodge the concepts from intimacy and merely institutionalize them. There is something unique and substantial about the way friendship as chosen family contains the variables to engage the living God and his transforming love.

In essence, the local church is made up of smaller chosen families that come together to emulate the Chosen Family of God.[3] Our marriages, children, and friendships are all different kinds of households that exist, not because of obligation, but because of the beauty of intentionally choosing each other. This is why marriages, families, and households are a picture of Christ and the church. To choose one another because God has chosen us, and to be in a covenantal, committed, intimate, proximate relationship with one another, is a beauty and wonder in and of itself. But it is also where we find the presence of God and live out the gospel together. It is where we learn the Story of God, and through that we can know who we are and live out of that identity.

This gathering of chosen family is also the very place that contains the mechanisms to combat the ills and idols of autonomy, entitlement, and productivity. To claim the local church as a kind of family means we need to re-evaluate some the programmatic approaches we have defaulted to. Joseph Hellerman writes in his book *When the Church Was a Family*:

> Now I find myself with increasing reservations about the wisdom of compartmentalizing God's family into separate fellowship groups according to life stages. I readily acknowledge the different needs of different age and interest groups in the church. Paul targeted instructions in his letters to specific groups of people, such as husbands and wives. Perhaps at some level there is a legitimate place for a life-stage approach to ministry. But it is clear that for Paul and the other early Christians there existed a focus of personal identity that was much bigger than one's life stage or marital state, namely, membership in the eternal family of God.[4]

There are certainly beneficial times and places for life-stage gatherings in a church. But we often do this because it is efficient and not because we have weighed the ramifications. Singles', married's, or children's gatherings are good so long as they do not break down the intergenerational, demographic-rich family identity and experience of the local church.

In a way, the basic structure of a family ideally provides the variables that make for a good church community. We need mothers and fathers. We need young people. Parents need grandparents and aunts and uncles for their kids. Married folks need single friends and friends with children or teenagers. Elderly folks need everyone. Children need everyone. We all need each other because we provide unique and beautiful components of a family. And when families are healthy, the presence of these generations and variations are the recipe for beautiful, fruitful, development.

We All Need Family

We don't all have family close by. And even if we do, sometimes our bio-families can be toxic or limited. My friend Jill has three young children. She and her husband do not live anywhere near their biological family. The idol of the nuclear family would say that all they need is each other, but she has felt the painful effects of isolation. They do a good job in providing for their kids and keeping a happy and balanced home life. But they are also taxed and exhausted. They do not have a relative nearby who can pick up the kids from school if a doctor's appointment runs late. And every time they want a date night, they must secure a babysitter and cover all the costs. The scope of parental influence for their kids is limited—there is no extended family member to provide that timely side-eye to a child who is being quietly mischievous.

Jill needs family.

I have another friend, Ellen, who is not married but lives with a roommate. The roommate relationship is friendly and amicable, but they both work long hours in different counties. Her bio-family is about an hour's drive away. But when she recently got a nail in her tire, she lamented the weight of her anxiety. Ironically, I found myself with a nail in my tire only a week after Ellen. But for me, the haunting questions of how to get it fixed, get to work, and pay for it all were met more easily with a spouse who teamed up with me to quickly create a plan. Like Ellen, I know little about cars and am grateful to have help when something goes wrong. But unlike my situation, Ellen had a more uphill battle to get through all the questions and needs that came from a simple nail in her tire.

Ellen needs family.

I have two mentors who have no close family nearby. Pamela is a cancer survivor who has battled many medical issues. She is in a wheelchair and requires help with daily tasks. But as they age and her husband, Victor, goes through his own health issues, their lives become complicated. After a successful surgery, Victor required a few weeks of recovery with limited physical activity or strain. Without the finances to afford a live-in nurse for those weeks, Pamela and Victor were anxiously planning for this situation through the help of generous neighbors and colleagues. But the circumstances left them both vulnerable and precarious.

Victor and Pamela need family.

But why would non-blood relatives aspire to these kinds of sacrifices? The types of help described here go well beyond bringing over a casserole or helping someone move. Friends are great for watching sports, playdates, and book clubs. A friend might even help you in a pinch or come watch your kid in an emergency. But the kind of friend whose dependability and intimacy allows for the proximity, commitment, and love needed by the people I mentioned, moves people into the realm of family. And we all need family.

When Jesus describes his disciples as his family, he is opening a new avenue for all of us to have family. If you have a solid relationship with your family of origin, great! They are also welcome into the family of God. But for the rest of us who may not be proximate to family geographically or relationally, there is a way forward to have a loving family in and through the local church.

We cannot simply relegate this idea of family to a merely spiritual concept. These intimacy motifs force us to reckon with flesh-and-blood as we learn the gospel in the thick of our own loneliness and brokenness. So if this chosen family identity is more than just a spiritual concept, how does it work?

Tables and Fires: The Art of Family Hospitality

The art of friendship is bound up in this identity as family. Families are not automatically healthy and life giving, yet ideologically, they contain a blueprint for how we love each other as friends. To unearth this blueprint, I start with the question: How does a family show hospitality to each other?

One of the more obvious and simple answers is: food. Families eat together.

Maybe not as much anymore, but the whole dining set up of any household points to the optimistic idea that we eat at least one daily meal with the other members of our household. Shared meals are still understood as a bonding point for families. The combination of time, attention, appetite, and intention is deeply valuable for families. It is no wonder that our sacrament of Christ's body and blood is often referred to as Communion or the Table. The history of the Eucharist and agape feast bring together this ritual gathering of the church family to eat and remember. Whether taking the Lord's Supper or attending the church potluck, there is a deep connection between the household meal and this practice in our church family. When these two overlap, we get moments where we share our household tables with each other and create a chosen family around them. Food, hospitality, and family have always been indelibly linked.

Literal feeding and metaphorical feeding are at the heart of being and healing as a community of friends-who-are-family. In his book *How to Stay Married*, Harrison Scott Key describes the actions of his local church and how important it was in helping him and his wife through some of the worst times of their lives. He explains it simply as:

> They hug us. They feed us. We feed them. They feed our children and we feed theirs and they feed [our dog] when we're out of town and when they're out of town, we feed their cats. All we're doing is feeding each other, basically, with hymns and prayers and sermons thrown in there to remind us why.[5]

I start this section on friendship-as-family-hospitality with the simplicity of eating together because beneath the simple act of a shared meal are layers of connection that turn strangers into friends and friends into family.

Another way families show hospitality to each other is through generosity. My parents used their resources to raise me. I was fed, clothed, and educated not because I entered the world deserving, but because I entered the world as a daughter. My parents' generosity and sharing of resources has never been a point of discussion, because no one ever needed to explain why a family would support each other with resources. We share a household and so we share a lot. We are a family.

In the same way, the family of God is called to a radical sharing of resources. The New Testament embodiment of the Old Testament Law on equity and generosity is a glaring example we would do well to take more seriously. Not everyone has a loving family to care for them when in financial need. Not everyone can move back home if they lose their job and suddenly can't pay the rent. And you do not need to be financially flush to be a blessing to your chosen family. The creativity of sharing what we have is just that; as a local church, we have the ability to see this come to life.

Solidarity and justice are other ways families show hospitality. Essentially, the hospitality of solidarity is getting to celebrate and mourn together. In the local church, this might already look like meals for new parents or even how we gather for funerals. But it can extend even further. The church I serve in has a moment each Sunday where we bless the wedding anniversaries of couples as well as birthdays that are being celebrated that week. But we also added a moment to celebrate milestones. The older single gentleman who will not celebrate a wedding anniversary gets to come up to celebrate his promotion at work. The young child comes up to celebrate getting a role in a local play. The young woman gets to celebrate three years of sobriety. And the church rejoices as one! We can create intentional space for this as we seek to show hospitality as a family.

Justice as hospitality is when families fight for each other. No one gets to pick on my little brother but me! Family members who might be our biggest critics can often turn on a dime and become ardent defenders when we face slander, exploitation, or injustice from outside forces. Justice shows up in families when there is an effort to repair something that has been broken. Adoption, as a legal and spiritual reality, is a prime example of how families exercise justice. There is something beautiful when we fight for each other under the banner of familial ties.

How then do we fight for each other as a chosen family? What would it look like to know our friends well enough to know when they need support against unjust forces? Not everyone has a family that will show up for them when they need support against the brokenness of this world. What about real injustices where we can bring resources and expertise to assist when there is no one else? I want those friends. I want to go to that church.

C. S. Lewis described the different Christian denominations as doors to rooms off a long hallway.[6] Each room would look different but there would be two things common to every room: a fire by which people are warmed and a table where people gather to eat and be nourished. Every denomination or local church, and every friendship, can seek these beautiful goals. Tables and fires. This is a fantastic summary of how the hospitality of families collides with the identity of the local church. In the local church we are not all blood relatives, so family must come through the avenue of friendship. Christ's friendship to us is what shows us the way.

The nourishment of those tables and the warmth of those fires can also be simply defined as a hospitality of care. This is where we find the nucleolus of intimacy once again. In a healthy family, there is a kind of intimacy whose motives are not questioned. When parents love their children, and children their siblings and parents, in the most ideal way, it is the kind of love and affection that is safe and beautiful. If the chosen family of the church were to aim for this kind of intimacy in friendship, then the ramifications would be life altering and life giving.

I have spoken with dozens of adults who are living or considering a celibate life and they wonder, *Is there a place for me in the local church?* I spoke with a friend recently who was lamenting something simple that many of us might take for granted. He felt the loss of a family dynamic in friendship in the expression of platonic but loving physical touch. He had a fraternal undergrad experience where his "brothers" were very comfortable giving each other hugs and showing brotherly affection. If you feel a certain knot even as you read this, it is likely a result of the hypersexualization that infects us all. We are skeptical of physical touch (many of us for good reason), and yet touch is vital to our humanity.

For men, this is a great challenge. It is no wonder C. S. Lewis dedicated so much of his chapter on friendship in *The Four Loves* to the subject of homophobia; we have made it nearly impossible in Western culture for our men to give and receive physical touch as an expression of friendship from other men. We have perpetuated a hypersexualization of their identities and lives as though every close contact must be sexual. It is as though their only acceptable physical outlets must be romantic or sexual. Everything else is suspect. My friend lamented the loss of this even as he became part of a pastoral staff of a large church. Days and weeks would go by without anything above a handshake. After such a positive experience of friendship for four years, he is beginning to see the degradative effects of this physical isolation. Where would it be possible to recapture a brotherhood and sisterhood that is safe and non-sexual? Could our chosen families provide this need without reducing people to sexual animals or objects?

We all need family.

We don't all have this with our biological family. And even if we do, we are not always guaranteed that they will be around or able to fulfill these needs. We need to expand our imagination about the spectrum of intimacy and recapture it as a family formed by the gospel. Benner says:

> Intimacy is shared experience. Jesus shared his experience with those who were his closest friends. And he invited them to accompany him as he walked through this experience. Intimacy can be experienced in a variety of forms. Two people are spiritually

intimate when they share spiritual experiences, emotionally intimate when they share emotional experiences, sexually intimate
when they share sexual experiences, and intellectually intimate
when they share intellectual experiences. . . . Spheres of intimacy
reinforce each other.[7]

All intimacy must be set by proper boundaries and built with a pattern
of trust. Remember, every intimate relationship requires communication
and trust-building behaviors with self-giving love, reciprocity, attention, curiosity, managing expectations, commitment, and mutuality. We cannot be
flippant with intimacy. Remember that its currency is vulnerability. So with
this in mind, what are the implications of a chosen family that shows hospitality not unlike a bio-family, tending to and caring about each other's needs?

Everyone gets a family.

Can you imagine! If our friendships in the local church were to do
something like this, everybody gets a family! The widowed, the divorced,
the struggling marriage, the person who lives alone, the elderly, the youth
not getting along with their parents; no one is left out. No one's value is
ranked based on their relationship status or age. No one must weather
the anxiety of getting a nail in their tire, being in between jobs, recovering alone from surgery, being isolated with the flu, or with three kids,
or with infertility, and we could go on and on. Everyone gets a family. Just
think about that for a moment. You can cancel street evangelism night and
your order for all those evangelism tracts. These tables and fires of the
grand hospitality of a chosen family would draw all to its warmth, light,
and nourishment. If biblical friendship is chosen family, then let's start
making some friends and build a family. Does your church facilitate this,
preach this, believe this?

The Alchemy of the Gospel

Okay, enough pie in the sky. Sure, it would be great if we all had friends
and family. It would be amazing if the local church really believed this

about our baptismal, ecclesial identity. But people are the worst, re-member? Our bio-fams might be rough but the same issues exist in people all around us. Choosing people is special but not a silver bullet. Plenty of people who chose to marry each other get divorced. Friends who choose each other one week will ghost each other the next. Parents who choose to have children do not always love them well. In fact, there really is no getting around the messiness of people and relationships. And there is no use trying to convince people that Christians are better parents, friends, spouses, or people just because they claim to follow Christ. Deep down, we believe Christians *should* be better at relationships. Yet there is a staggering amount of evidence to the contrary.

The ancient concept of alchemy was belief in a chemical marvel that could turn lead into gold. It feels a bit fantastical like Rumpelstiltskin spinning straw into gold, but for a long time there was a scientific fas-cination with the possibility that chemistry could provide this transfor-mation and make the world rich. But this alchemy never came true. Gold remained gold and lead remained lead. That was it.

I know this is how we often feel about the mess of our intimate relation-ships. It's as though all the best practices, researched studies, and advice can't overcome the stubborn relentlessness of sin and shame.

But friends, I believe that the gospel is alchemy.

The forces of deceit, fear, sin, and shame are very powerful. We need to know that there is something even more powerful and captivating that can overcome these forces and bring us home to our identities in Christ. Henri Nouwen knew the heights of prestige and the depths of loneliness. He writes:

> It requires discipline to come home and listen, especially when our fears are so noisy that they keep driving us outside of ourselves. But when we grasp the truth that we already have a home, we may at last have the strength to unmask the illusions created by our fears and continue to return again and again and again.[8]

Like Jill Pole when she first meets Aslan in *The Silver Chair*, her fear of the lion is intense, but her thirst is even greater.[9] And so even though she is terrified of being attacked by a lion, she steps closer and closer to the river running behind him. Our thirst for intimacy can be cheapened and distorted only to drive us deeper into deceit, fear, sin, and shame. But when we learn that our thirst for intimacy is part of the Story we have been called into, it becomes an avenue by which we find our way home to ourselves in Christ again and again.

To do this we become students of the gospel. We must become chronic grace givers and grace receivers. And this gives us the freedom to be vulnerable and build trust. We can connect instead of isolate. We can share instead of hide. We can be empowered and accepted. "We can live together in this home without asking for much more than a willingness to constantly confess our weaknesses to each other and to always forgive each other," Nouwen says.[10] And along the way, our dead lumps of lead are turned to gold.

Anyone can follow the best practices of self-giving, attention, reciprocity, commitment, mutuality, and the like and have healthy relationships. They are available to everyone regardless of what they believe about God. With these gifts of common grace, we can have sustainable relationships. But that is all. Is there more?

If we want to access pure freedom and fullness in an identity secured for us by the Love that created the universe, we need the gospel. Nouwen notes: "God alone is free enough from wounds to offer us a fearless place. In and through God we can be faithful to each other: in friendship, marriage, and community. This intimate bond with God, constantly nurtured by prayer, offers us a true home."[11] With God, we get to know the Story that provides the framework and purposes of our story. We can have healthy relationships that are born of a transformative sanctification in intimacy. All our mess and brokenness is somehow and miraculously turned into gold. Beauty for ashes, darkness that is light, gardens in deserts. This is the alchemy of God. And we are all invited to participate in this difficult, beautiful journey.

The local church can be the greenhouse for a theology of intimacy when we, first, prioritize the gospel as it is woven with the Story of God and intimate relationships. Second, when church is a proximate, safe, embodied experience that, third, embraces its identity as the family of God. As Myles Werntz says:

> It is thus not only a matter of explicitly stating our doctrine concerning what the church is; the habits of our gathering of singing, praying, working, and reading Scripture are changed. For when we turn to the days in which we live separate from one another, falling back into isolation is easy; unless these acts become movements within the soul, we will neither yearn for our lives together nor see our times separated from one another as any real loss. But if cultivated and ingrained into the practice of communities, these habits emanate out into the days in which we are scattered into the world.[12]

To my brothers and sisters in the local church, will our churches be the place where we inspire healthy intimate relationships, without hierarchy, because they are tied to engagement of the gospel together as a family? We must reflect on our acquiescence to cultural liturgies and narratives that infest our theology of intimacy. Our churches should be places that push back against autonomy, entitlement, and productivity. We must be a people who invite each other to know our true value and identity as Christ's beloveds in relationship with him and each other.

The Storytellers

I began with a challenge to ask better questions. We all have questions about relationships, and we are often unaware that many of these questions are tethered to our ideas and conceptions about God and ourselves. I would never belittle or dismiss the questions that drive students to my office. Jettie sincerely wanted a thriving relationship with God, and she also desperately wanted someone to want her, see her, and date her. None of these are unimportant matters. But our approach to helping people like Jettie often comes from a detachment of how her story is part of the Story. We may strive to help someone like Jettie without ever drawing them to the warmth, nourishment, and truths of Christ and his redemptive mission that they are a part of.

We need to ask better questions that get to the thing under the thing. Where is deceit, fear, sin, or shame? Are there lies feeding on someone's identity that have blinded them to who they are or who God is? Do they know why and for what purpose they seek intimacy? Do they know they are created for intimacy?

I hope these chapters have given you hope and encouragement. I hope they have drawn you to the life-giving gospel of our Savior and offered fresh insights to the gospel tapestry woven with threads of intimacy. I hope those of you who are practitioners, parents, or other guides feel more equipped to ask better questions when presented with relationship complexities. I hope you see the importance of friendship and are dedicated to flattening the artificial, relational hierarchies we have adopted from culture. I hope my friends of color will create more content on gospel-centric intimate relationships. I want my students to not end up like Hudson and others who feel that these resources are not for them. We need you and your voices.

I hope church leaders will lean less on programs and more on hospitality as the avenue to recapture our identity as a chosen family in the local church. I hope your people all find friendship and family under your servanthood. I hope to see books and sermons about intimate relationships that don't just offer advice but lead the reader or listener toward our living Savior, Jesus Christ.

And I hope we all have immersed even deeper into the life-giving truths of the gospel. If these pages have been a small community of remembrance for you, it is all worth it.

To return to Lauren Winner's framework, I want to encourage us all to move away from being police or sentimentalists about intimate relationships. We do not need legalism or licentiousness. Neither have proven to be true avenues to healthy relationships or identity. But we can be storytellers. We can be individuals whose collective voices and lived relationships embody and tell the Story of God. As Curt Thompson reminds us, "Because shame is an embodied affect, we need more than facts in order to undermine it."[13] There is a power in presence that no words on a page, doctrines, advice, or concepts can match. Perhaps this is why God chose intimate relationships as the conduit for his gospel and himself. Through incarnation, indwelling, and choosing, he is the embodiment and invitation of fullness, freedom, and love. Our relationships become both the ends *and* the means of experiencing God and his good news.

The key to healthy, intimate relationships is a recapturing of the gospel. As we move forward to address the pressing questions about our love life, families, and friendships, may our way always draw us closer to Christ, our true north. This way will always lead us home to each other, ourselves, and our Savior.

A Messy Hope

"It's 6:00 a.m., we can probably call Barrett."

I say this to my husband, Mike, after many long moments of silence. We had been out on our front porch together in our pajamas since 4:00 a.m., since the break-in occurred.

We awoke in the early morning hours to our home alarm going off. It had been a long, hot summer day and we had forgotten to close and lock one of our small living room windows. We had had break-ins before but never while we were home. On this evening, a burglar—we would later find out had already robbed half of our neighborhood—squeezed through our open window and was inside our house. But he set off a motion sensor and panicked. In his panic, and drug-induced lack of judgment, he escaped our home by going headfirst through the kitchen window above our sink.

When the police arrived, we were instructed to stay outside our house, now a crime scene with evidence, and wait for the one crime unit in all of Nashville-Davidson County to come and process the blood and finger-prints. It would take them until 11:00 a.m. to arrive at our house.

Meanwhile, we were sequestered on our front porch.

The first two hours, we just sat in shock. The whole incident had scared us in ways we had never experienced. It would take years to process the trauma of this moment. But at 6:00 a.m., I realized it was Sunday morning and our friend Barrett, who is an insomniac obsessed with physical fitness, would likely be up to go for a morning run before church. Mike called him. Sure enough, he was up and said he would come straight over.

In a few minutes, not only was Barrett on the porch with us, but he brought us coffee and breakfast. He also brought his laptop. He remembered that I was in grad school at the time and would need to email my professors. He did not know that our laptops had been stolen in the robbery, but his instinct to help preempted my own thought to ask. I was able to contact all my professors that very morning because of his thoughtfulness.

He sat with us, listened to us, and cried with us. As the morning reached a reasonable hour, he called in the cavalry.

By the time the crime-scene unit left, we had close to a dozen of our friends at our home. They swept up glass and helped clean fingerprinting dust from all our surfaces (not easy!). They stayed with us all day. They watched movies with us until we felt safe enough to fall asleep in our bedroom. They came and checked on us the next day and sent texts, food, and support for the weeks to come.

These friends jumped right into action because they were more than friends. They were our family.

We had moved to Nashville six years earlier knowing almost no one. Through our church, we met a number of people and we became a small group. During those years, this group evolved in ways we could never have predicted. This was our first introduction to adult friendship that lived out the hospitality of a family.

Our little group helped each other financially. We built porches together. Babysat for free. Vacationed together. We studied Scripture together and attended church together. We laughed uncontrollably when our preacher accidently said in a sermon that we need to "nail our junk to the cross." We volunteered together. We hosted game nights, birthdays, girls/guys outings, and holiday events. We wept over miscarriages, jobs lost, and family trauma. We helped pack and move some of them when life called them elsewhere. It was no shock to Mike or me when they came to our home on that dreadful morning.

But that morning was also the first time it really occurred to me that these beloved friends were actually family, living out the gospel together. We did not have any relatives within a three-hour drive of us, but that did not mean that we did not need family. These friends, they were our family.

I've seen this theology of intimacy work in my life right in front of my eyes. I believe, with all my heart, that if we (1) get honest about the syncretism and cultural liturgies that have infected our theology of intimacy, (2) actively dismantle these myths in our communities, and (3) seek the intimate relationships we are made for with the gospel as our aim and source, then we can fight the tide of isolation and discover healthy, intimate relationships. Everyone should have intimacy (whether you are married or not) and we can experience deep, meaningful intimacy with or without sex.

But there are no platitudes or simple examples of gospel-centered relationships that this book can contain. In fact, our desire to use books like this to paint tidy, contained, pictures of healthy, flourishing households and communities is exactly what gives us false expectations when we find our own realities so disappointing.

I would like to offer something else instead: a messy hope.

Our little Nashville family of friends had several wonderful years together, but eventually things fell apart and several of those couples don't even speak to each other anymore. There were divorces, offenses, and just general relocation that finally drew the group to a close. Since then, I have been looking for something like that experience, with little luck.

But the fact that it ever happened in the first place is a miracle. And when we have the joy of building new friendship-to-family opportunities, it will also be a miracle. The Holy Spirit is on the move. God desires that you and I have intimate relationships in communities of gospel remembrance.

But we will need some help along this journey. This book is a start. It is meant to orient us away from the toxic fundamentals we have been clinging to and recalibrate our compasses. Now we know that we are created for intimacy, and that the purpose of these relationships is not to cure our loneliness, but to reveal God and the gospel in an embodied, sanctifying experience of love and grace. Now that we have this foundation, it is your turn: you can be people who seek healthy, sustainable relationships by centering the gospel, exposing lies, clinging to grace, and claiming your part in communities of gospel remembrance.

But let's start here, with our messy hope and restored theology of intimacy. You are created to know God and others deeply and to be deeply known by them. Let's begin together to call our relationships back to the gospel and move forward in the hope that God is working, even now, in our beautiful, messy lives.

Acknowledgments

I am deeply grateful to Al Hsu, Cindy Bunch, and InterVarsity Press, who took a chance on me. It is a dream come true to work with you all, a dream first made possible by my bishop, Todd Hunter. To the clergy in my diocese: thanks to all who have given advice and encouragement along the way.

I am grateful for my Baylor colleagues who also encouraged this book: University Chaplain Burt Burleson, Spiritual Life, Student Life, and wider Baylor colleagues who invited me to speak or present on the content. Especially Malcolm Foley and our First-Time Authors Club. (Go buy Malcolm's book!)

Love and gratitude to my All Saints Waco family. I love being your deacon and friend. And love for the greater Waco establishments that (unknowingly) supported this book. Pages were written in Pinewood Coffee & Pub, Fabled Bookstore, World Cup Café (shout out to my Saturday morning crew!), Dichotomy, Street Dog Café, and Z's at the Curry.

My research was birthed from the community of Trinity Anglican Seminary: my Doktorvaters Wes Hill, Jack Gabig, and Laurie Thompson and the community at TAS. But special thanks to Ellen, Nicole, Lee-Anna, and Linda.

My affection and gratitude will always be with the students I got to minister to and with during my years as a chaplain at Berry College. A special thanks goes out to the students who agreed to participate in my research as subjects; you know who you are. Thanks to Whit Whitaker and Jon Huggins for all the support. To Susan Conradson, and The Bissonettes for the love, support, and long hours of conversation.

This manuscript was a true team effort: thank you, Blake Dean. You are like a brother to me. May the trail of spilled coffee always lead us back to one another. Thank you Mallory Ellington for also being witness and comrade from the early days of this project. Thank you for lending your stories and allowing your life to be lived out loud in all its pain and beauty. Thank you Joao, Grillo Moraes, Zion Brown, and Erin Dean for your friendship and support. This book is indelibly marked with "the Joao of it all " and Z with the miles we walked together. Erin Dean, may there always be a donut or Chick-fil-A along the way. And to Matthew and Kathryn Aughtry, who helped me come up with bad titles and great content. For endless evenings together with conversation, good drinks, and occasional pipe tobacco. For embodying the friendship that is family.

Thank you, Mom and Dad. Your prayers kept me safe. I am indebted to our friends from our years in Nashville (POC and Midtown Fellowship!) and especially Jill and Clayton Altom for efforts that sustain our friendship.

To my amazing husband, Mike: thank you for your love and support through my master's, job searches, ordination, doctorate, moving halfway across the country, and this book. You are the silent author of this work, and no one will ever know how much of your wisdom and life are on these pages because of your relentless support and care. I love you back.

Questions for Reflection and Discussion

1. Defining Intimate Relationships

1. "I can live without sex, but I cannot live without intimacy." What is your initial response to this statement? Skepticism? Intrigue? Hope? Talk about what this statement elicits in you and why. Encourage others in the group to share about their history with concepts like this one.

2. Should Christians be better at relationships than non-Christians? Why or why not?

3. What are some of your top questions about relationships? Take a moment to muse on what might be driving these questions. What do they reveal about your own ideas about intimacy?

4. Review the diagram for the fundamentals of intimacy. What do you think about this summary? What sticks out to you? What might be examples that come to mind of people or situations that embody different fundamentals from the diagram?

2. How the Western World Co-opted Our Identities

1. What are some examples from books, shows, movies, or other popular media that have been formative for your own ideas about relationship?

2. How has romance idolatry or hypersexuality affected your own life?

3. What is the role of technology in your relationships? How has it helped or hurt?

3. How Christendom Baptized Secularization

1. If you grew up in a Christian context, what are some of the resources or people who shaped your view of faith and intimacy—both helpful and harmful?

2. Can you name some secular, cultural ideas that seeped into your own engagement with Christendom and relationships?

3. In your opinion, what is the connection between good behaviors in intimate relationships and growing in maturity in faith?

4. Our Broken Compasses and the Role of Grace

1. What is your initial response to the summaries for culture and Christendom in the realm of intimacy? Do you agree or disagree, and why?

2. How did you feel about the responses from the focus groups?

3. "Whether we are getting our information from inside or outside our faith contexts, all the narratives are attempting to ascribe identity and value through intimacy, statuses, and behaviors." What messages have you absorbed about your worth or identity in the presence or absence of your relationships? Where did these messages come from and why are they important to you?

4. When have you experienced grace in your life?

5. Discovering the Origins of Intimacy and Our Desires

1. In relationships, have you ever felt like you have exhausted all the variables that are in your control? Describe the areas where you hope for divine intervention or help.

2. "You are created for intimacy." How does this statement make you feel? Do you agree or disagree? What are the implications?

3. If the origins of intimacy are of goodness and connection, and not about our lack or loneliness, what does this shift about your own ideas about relationships? Are you, like Jettie, driven by your ache?

4. "When we learn that our desire for sex, companionship, friendship, family, and deep connection is an essential component of the Story of God and Christ's redemptive work in the world, we read the very pages that will tell us who we are." In your opinion, what does this statement mean?

6. Deceit, Sin, Fear, and Shame: Why We Can't Seem to Make Good Choices

1. How has shame played a role in your history of intimacy?

2. Vulnerability is necessary but risky. In what ways can you build safe avenues of trust for vulnerability in relationships?

3. Do you tend to risk vulnerability too soon or do you tend to withhold yourself even if trust is built? Why do you suppose you have this tendency?

7. Knowing and Being Known Through the Three Intimacy Motifs

1. What does it mean to have a relationship with God? What are the concepts and stories of how this reality shows up in your own life?

2. What does intimacy have to do with the gospel?

3. Where have you witnessed restoring, gifting, or abiding in your walk with God? What does it mean to you that God chooses you and will never leave you in isolation or scarcity?

8. Loneliness and the Location of God

1. If intimacy is the enemy of shame, what does this look like in your own life? How does a move toward intimacy dismantle the shame, sin, and fear we carry?

2. We can often pull away from people while we work on ourselves or get right enough to be in a relationship, but how is God calling us to find sanctification in and through our relationships?

3. What is your own experience with loneliness and isolation?

4. What are examples of healthy solitude?

9. The Gospel Community of Remembrance

1. Have you ever placed a weight of expectations on a relationship to cure your loneliness or shame?

2. What are some of the lies you are prone to believe about yourself that run counter to the gospel, but are difficult to shake? What does the gospel say about you that is counter to these lies?

3. Why is it so difficult to remember what is true about God and our identity? What ways, explicitly and implicitly, can we preach and embody this truth to each other in our relationships?

4. What do you need to hear God say to you about who you are?

10. Examining Intimacy in Our Gospel Communities

1. What is your experience with the local church? Have you observed relational hierarchies?

2. What are your initial thoughts about romance idolatry and idolatry of the nuclear family in churches?

3. "Friendship, not romance, marriage, or the nuclear family, is the hub of the intimacy motifs that secures and elevates all three of them." What are your thoughts on this claim? How important is the art of friendship in relation to the other spheres of intimacy?

11. The Art of Friendship and the Family of God

1. What is your experience with family? Are you close relationally or geographically to your family? Have you experienced chosen family?

2. If the biblical picture of friendship is family, what does this mean for your current friendships?

3. Hospitality is outlined in five categories: eating, generosity, solidarity, justice, and care. What sticks out to you and why? How are your friendships championing these categories? What categories need improvement?

4. The gospel takes messy, broken people and transforms them into family. How do you see this, or hope for this, in your relationships and yourself?

Notes

1. Defining Intimate Relationships

[1]While the data is not identical, the consistency of findings given the variety of research centers and the range of years when studies were conducted is enough to show that divorce rates are not stymied by Christian faith nor is the longevity of marriage enhanced by it. Here are a few sources: "Religious Landscape Study," Pew Research Center, accessed September 9, 2024, www.pewresearch.org/religion/religious-landscape -study/; Lyman Stone and Brad Wilcox, "The Religious Marriage Paradox: Younger Marriage, Less Divorce," *Institute for Family Studies*, December 15, 2021, https:// ifstudies.org/blog/the-religious-marriage-paradox-younger-marriage-less-divorce; Mark A. Smith, "Religion, Divorce, and the Missing Culture War in America," *Political Science Quarterly (Academy of Political Science)* 125, no. 1 (2010): 57-85, https://doi .org/10.1002/j.1538-165X.2010.tb00668.x.

[2]"Religion's Relationship to Happiness, Civic Engagement and Health Around the World," Pew Research Center, January 31, 2019, www.pewresearch.org/religion/2019 /01/31/religions-relationship-to-happiness-civic-engagement-and-health-around-the -world/.

[3]David Brooks, *How to Know a Person: The Art of Seeing Others Deeply and Being Deeply Seen* (New York: Random House, 2023), 87.

[4]Lauren F. Winner, *Real Sex: The Naked Truth about Chastity* (Grand Rapids, MI: Brazos Press, 2005), 51-52.

[5]Rowland Miller, *Intimate Relationships* (New York: McGraw Hill, 2017); Caryl E. Rusbult et al., "Accommodation Processes in Close Relationships: Theory and Preliminary Empirical Evidence," *Journal of Personality and Social Psychology* 60, no. 1 (1991): 53-78, https://doi.org/10.1037/0022-3514.60.1.53; John H. Harvey and Julia Omarzu, "Minding the Close Relationship," *Personality & Social Psychology Review (Lawrence Erlbaum Associates)* 1, no. 3 (1997): 224, https://doi.org/10.1207 /s15327957pspr0103_3; Dalmas A. Taylor, "The Development of Interpersonal

Relationships: Social Penetration Processes," *Journal of Social Psychology* 75, no. 1 (1968): 79-90, https://doi.org/10.1080/00224545.1968.9712476.

2. How the Western World Co-opted Our Identities

[1]Wendell Berry, *Sex, Economy, Freedom & Community: Eight Essays* (New York: Pantheon, 1993), 113-14.

[2]"No, It's Not Selfish to Want to Go on a Spiritual Journey," Oprah.com, accessed September 9, 2024, www.oprah.com/inspiration/elizabeth-gilbert-taking-a-spiritual -journey; Maureen Callahan, "Inside Elizabeth Gilbert's Self-Help Long Con," June 4, 2019, https://nypost.com/2019/06/04/eat-pray-lose-inside-elizabeth-gilberts -self-help-long-con/.

[3]Peter Augustine Lawler, *Modern and American Dignity: Who We Are as Persons, and What That Means for Our Future* (Wilmington, DE: ISI Books, 2010), 76.

[4]Lawler, *Modern and American Dignity*, 196-97.

[5]"Cities Where Work from Home Has Declined," LLC.Org, December 6, 2023, www .llc.org/work-from-home-decline/; Roy Maurer, "Job Seekers Crave Remote Work, Even as Remote Jobs Decline," SHRM, January 24, 2024, www.shrm.org/topics -tools/news/talent-acquisition/remote-jobs-decline-new-hires-return-to-office.

[6]Karen Doyle, "Here's How Often Americans Move—And How Much They're Spending," GOBankingRates.com, December 29, 2023, www.gobankingrates.com /investing/real-estate/how-often-americans-move-how-much-theyre-spending/.

[7]Jean M. Twenge, *Generation Me: Why Today's Young Americans Are More Confident, Assertive, Entitled—and More Miserable Than Ever Before* (New York: Simon and Schuster, 2006), 156.

[8]Sarah Coakley, *The New Asceticism* (London: Bloomsbury Continuum, 2015), 9.

[9]Though the statement came first from St. Augustine, Smith's book translates this important concept for modern readers. James K. A. Smith, *You Are What You Love: The Spiritual Power of Habit* (Grand Rapids, MI: Brazos Press, 2016).

[10]Donna Freitas, *The End of Sex: How Hookup Culture Is Leaving a Generation Unhappy, Sexually Unfulfilled, and Confused About Intimacy* (New York: Basic Books, 2013), 31.

[11]Freitas, *The End of Sex*, 11.

[12]The concept of "romance idolatry" originates with Pieter Valk and his observations influenced by Kutter Callaway, *Breaking the Marriage Idol: Reconstructing Our Cultural and Spiritual Norms* (Downers Grove, IL: InterVarsity Press, 2018). Valk popularized this concept in his article, Pieter Valk and Kutter Callaway, "A Pandemic of Romantic Idolatry," Christ and Pop Culture, July 13, 2022, https://christandpop culture.com/a-pandemic-of-romantic-idolatry/.

[13]Claire Mortimer, *Romantic Comedy*, Routledge Film Guidebooks (Oxford: Routledge, 2010).

[14]Dimitrije Curcic, "Fiction Books Sales Statistics," WordsRated, January 30, 2023, https://wordsrated.com/fiction-books-sales/.

[15]Coakley, *The New Asceticism*, 4.

[16]Zachary Wagner, *Non-Toxic Masculinity: Recovering Healthy Male Sexuality* (Downers Grove, IL: InterVarsity Press, 2023), 49.

[17]Luke Barr and Meredith Deliso, "Ohio 'Incel' Pleads Guilty to Plotting Mass Shooting Against Women at University: DOJ," *ABC News*, October 12, 2022, https://abcnews.go.com/US/ohio-incel-pleads-guilty-plotting-mass-shooting-women/story?id=91388041.

[18]Mark Travers, "A Psychologist Breaks Down the Storm That Creates 'Incel' Men–And Offers a Solution," *Forbes*, April 10, 2023, www.forbes.com/sites/traversmark/2023/04/10/a-psychologist-breaks-down-the-storm-that-creates-incel-men--and-offers-a-solution/.

[19]Freitas, *The End of Sex*, 15.

[20]Sherry Turkle, *Alone Together* (New York: Basic Books, 2017), 227-28.

[21]Twenge, *Generation Me*, 150.

[22]Turkle, *Alone Together*, 1.

[23]Turkle, *Alone Together*, xii.

[24]"YouTubers Cheer People Up More than Casual Friends, Study Suggests," *ScienceDaily*, May 23, 2024, www.sciencedaily.com/releases/2024/05/240523112500.htm.

[25]Turkle, *Alone Together*, 227-28, 492.

[26]Vivek H. Murthy, "Our Epidemic of Loneliness and Isolation," *The U.S. Surgeon General's Advisory on the Healing Effects of Social Connection and Community 2023*, accessed September 9, 2024, www.hhs.gov/sites/default/files/surgeon-general-social-connection-advisory.pdf.

[27]Berry, *Sex, Economy, Freedom & Community*, 143.

[28]Berry, *Sex, Economy, Freedom & Community*, 13.

3. How Christendom Baptized Secularization

[1]Dolly Parton, *Dream More: Celebrate the Dreamer in You* (New York: Riverhead Trade, 2013), 91.

[2]Erin Moniz, "Created to Connect: A Gospel Understanding of Intimacy for Emerging Adults in a College Setting," Trinity Library Thesis Collection, 2021. All participant quotes come from the research published in this thesis.

[3]This "dawn of the Christian-industrial complex" is in reference to the documented boom of Christian bookstores opening across North America between 1975 and 1985. No, I won't tell you how old I was when this happened.

[4]Myles Werntz, *From Isolation to Community: A Renewed Vision for Christian Life Together* (Grand Rapids, MI: Baker Academic, 2022), 8.

[5]Joseph H. Hellerman, *When the Church Was a Family: Recapturing Jesus' Vision for Authentic Christian Community* (Nashville, TN: B&H Academic, 2009), 143.

[6]Lauren F. Winner, *Real Sex: The Naked Truth about Chastity* (Grand Rapids, MI: Brazos Press, 2005), 52.

[7]Daniel J. Brendsel, "Cutting the Fruit While Watering the Root: Selfies, Sexuality and the Sensibilities of the American Church," in *Beauty, Order, and Mystery: A Christian Vision of Human Sexuality*, ed. Gerald L. Hiestand and Todd Wilson (Downers Grove, IL: InterVarsity Press, 2017), 82.

[8]Sheila Wray Gregoire, Rebecca Gregoire Lindenbach, and Joanna Sawatsky, *The Great Sex Rescue: The Lies You've Been Taught and How to Recover What God Intended* (Grand Rapids, MI: Baker Books, 2021); Zachary Wagner, *Non-Toxic Masculinity: Recovering Healthy Male Sexuality* (Downers Grove, IL: InterVarsity Press, 2023).

[9]Gregoire, Lindenbach, and Sawatsky, *The Great Sex Rescue*, 115.

[10]Sarah Coakley, *The New Asceticism* (London: Bloomsbury Continuum, 2015), 12.

[11]Gregoire, Lindenbach, and Sawatsky, *The Great Sex Rescue*, 154-55.

[12]Hellerman, *When the Church Was a Family*, 91.

[13]Stanley Hauerwas and Bishop William H. Willimon, *Resident Aliens: Life in the Christian Colony* (Nashville, TN: Abingdon Press, 2014), 138.

4. Our Broken Compasses and the Role of Grace

[1]G. K. Chesterton, *The Defendant*, ed. Dale Ahlquist (Mineola, NY: Dover, 2012), 18.

[2]John H. Harvey and Julia Omarzu, "Minding the Close Relationship," *Personality & Social Psychology Review (Lawrence Erlbaum Associates)* 1, no. 3 (1997): 224, https://doi.org/10.1207/s15327957pspr0103_3.

[3]Sheila Wray Gregoire, Rebecca Gregoire Lindenbach, and Joanna Sawatsky, *The Great Sex Rescue: The Lies You've Been Taught and How to Recover What God Intended* (Grand Rapids, MI: Baker Books, 2021), 158.

[4]Jean M. Twenge, *Generation Me: Why Today's Young Americans Are More Confident, Assertive, Entitled—and More Miserable Than Ever Before* (New York: Simon and Schuster, 2006), 210.

[5]Gregoire, Lindenbach, and Sawatsky, *The Great Sex Rescue*.

[6]Gregoire, Lindenbach, and Sawatsky, *The Great Sex Rescue*.

[7]John M. Gottman et al., "Predicting Marital Happiness and Stability from Newlywed Interactions," *Journal of Marriage and Family* 60, no. 1 (1998): 5-22, https://doi.org/10.2307/353438.; Elizabeth Beyer, ed., *Created to Thrive: Cultivating Abuse-Free Faith Communities* (Minneapolis, MN: CBE International, 2021).

[8]Lauren F. Winner, *Real Sex: The Naked Truth about Chastity* (Grand Rapids, MI: Brazos Press, 2005), 30.

5. Discovering the Origins of Intimacy and Our Desires

[1]Curt Thompson, *The Soul of Desire: Discovering the Neuroscience of Longing, Beauty, and Community* (Downers Grove, IL: InterVarsity Press, 2021), 21.

[2]Thompson, *The Soul of Desire*, 36.

[3]One modern attempt that grapples with this is the book *The Right to Sex* by Amia Srinivasan (New York: Farrar, Straus and Giroux, 2021).

[4]Fred Sanders, *The Triune God*, eds. Michael Allen and Scott R. Swain (Grand Rapids, MI: Zondervan, 2016), 132.

[5]Michael Reeves, *Delighting in the Trinity: An Introduction to the Christian Faith* (Downers Grove, IL: IVP Academic, 2012), 102. While this is true, it is important to note that this theology of relationship is not explicitly stated in Scripture. Theology is done at the concept level, not at the word level. While there are no explicit words in Scripture that state this doctrine, the concept of intimacy clearly is assumed throughout Scripture as God continues to reveal himself in covenant relationship with his people.

[6]Fred Sanders, *The Deep Things of God: How the Trinity Changes Everything*, 2nd ed. (Wheaton, IL: Crossway, 2017), 86.

[7]Thompson, *The Soul of Desire*, 6.

[8]Thompson, *The Soul of Desire*, 6.

[9]C. S. Lewis, *The Four Loves* (San Francisco: HarperOne, 2017), 2-3.

[10]Michael D. Williams, *Far as the Curse Is Found: The Covenant Story of Redemption* (Phillipsburg, NJ: P & R Publishing, 2005), 38.

[11]Curt Thompson, *The Soul of Shame: Retelling the Stories We Believe About Ourselves* (Downers Grove, IL: InterVarsity Press, 2015), 121-22.

[12]Maria L. Boccia, "Human Interpersonal Relationships and Love of the Trinity," *Priscilla Papers* 25, no. 4 (2011): 22-26.

[13]Boccia, "Human Interpersonal Relationships."

[14]Lewis, *The Four Loves*, 129.

6. Deceit, Sin, Fear, and Shame: Why We Can't Seem to Make Good Choices

[1]Michael Ende, *The Neverending Story*, trans. Ralph Manheim (New York: Dutton Books for Young Readers, 1997), 147.

[2]Ende, *The Neverending Story*, 148.

[3]Curt Thompson, *The Soul of Shame: Retelling the Stories We Believe About Ourselves* (Downers Grove, IL: InterVarsity Press, 2015), 66.

[4]Brené Brown, *Rising Strong: How the Ability to Reset Transforms the Way We Live, Love, Parent, and Lead* (New York: Random House, 2017), 194.

[5]Thompson, *The Soul of Shame*, 63.

[6]Curt Thompson, *The Soul of Desire: Discovering the Neuroscience of Longing, Beauty, and Community* (Downers Grove, IL: InterVarsity Press, 2021), 22.

[7]Thompson, *The Soul of Shame*, 62.

[8]Brown, *Rising Strong*, 195.

[9]Henri J. M. Nouwen, *Lifesigns: Intimacy, Fecundity, and Ecstasy in Christian Perspective* (New York: Image, 1989), 30.

[10]Brown, *Rising Strong*, xvii.

[11]Thompson, *The Soul of Shame*, 99.

[12]C. S. Lewis, *The Four Loves* (San Francisco: HarperOne, 2017), 121.

7. Knowing and Being Known Through the Three Intimacy Motifs

[1]Preston Sprinkle, "Is Jesus My Boyfriend?," *Theology in the Raw*, February 24, 2015, https://theologyintheraw.com/is-jesus-my-boyfriend/.

[2]Henri J. M. Nouwen, *Lifesigns: Intimacy, Fecundity, and Ecstasy in Christian Perspective* (New York: Image, 1989), 41.

[3]Thomas R. Schreiner, Miles V. Van Pelt, and Dane C. Ortlund, *Covenant and God's Purpose for the World* (Wheaton, IL: Crossway, 2017), 13.

[4]Michael D. Williams, *Far as the Curse Is Found: The Covenant Story of Redemption* (Phillipsburg, NJ: P & R Publishing, 2005), 38.

[5]Michael Horton, *Introducing Covenant Theology* (Grand Rapids, MI: Baker Books, 2009), 9.

[6]Shel Silverstein, *The Giving Tree* (New York: HarperCollins, 1964).

[7]John E. Colwell, "A Conversation Overheard: Reflecting on the Trinitarian Grammar of Intimacy and Substance," *Evangelical Quarterly* 86, no. 1 (2014): 75.

[8]Joel R. Beeke and Paul M. Smalley, "Images of Union and Communion with Christ," *Puritan Reformed Journal* 8, no. 2 (2016): 125-36.

[9]Beeke and Smalley, "Images of Union and Communion with Christ," 129.

[10]C. S. Lewis, "Letter to Father Peter Bide on 4/29/1959," in *The Collected Letters of C. S. Lewis, Volume 3: Narnia, Cambridge, and Joy, 1950–1963* (San Francisco: HarperOne, 2007), 132.

[11]Michael Horton, *Rediscovering the Holy Spirit: God's Perfecting Presence in Creation, Redemption, and Everyday Life* (Grand Rapids, MI: Zondervan, 2017), 45.

8. Loneliness and the Location of God

[1]Curt Thompson, *The Soul of Shame: Retelling the Stories We Believe About Ourselves* (Downers Grove, IL: InterVarsity Press, 2015), 183.

[2]Henri J. M. Nouwen, *Lifesigns: Intimacy, Fecundity, and Ecstasy in Christian Perspective* (New York: Image, 1989), 43.

[3]Sherry Turkle, *Alone Together* (New York: Basic Books, 2017), 43.

[4]Anna J. Finley and Stacey M. Schaefer, "Affective Neuroscience of Loneliness: Potential Mechanisms Underlying the Association between Perceived Social Isolation, Health, and Well-Being," *Journal of Psychiatry and Brain Science* 7, no. 6 (2022): https://doi.org/10.20900/jpbs.20220011.

[5]Henri J. M. Nouwen, *Intimacy* (San Francisco: Harper & Row, 1981), 35.

[6]Turkle, *Alone Together*, 285.

9. The Gospel Community of Remembrance

[1]Fiona Roberts, "'He Ate His First Seafood in 25 Years': Homeless Man Off the Streets After Brother Leaves Him Entire $100k Estate," Mail Online, June 19, 2011, www.dailymail.co.uk/news/article-2005476/Homeless-man-told-rich-Lawyers-track-Max-Melitzer-huge-inheritance.html.

[2]Stanley Hauerwas, *Christian Existence Today: Essays on Church, World, and Living in Between* (Eugene, Oregon: Wipf & Stock, 2010), 103-4.

[3]If you are not sure who you are because of the redemption of God through Christ and the Holy Spirit, these verses provide a list of values and promises that define who God is and who we are: Genesis 26:3, 24; 28:15; Exodus 3:12; 6:6-7; 34:6; Leviticus 26:12; Numbers 14:18; Deuteronomy 20:1; 31:6; Joshua 1:9; 2 Samuel 7:24; 2 Chronicles 13:12; 32:7; Nehemiah 9:17; Psalm 46:7; 103:8; 139:11-12; 145:8; Isaiah 9:2; 41:10; 43:2; 52:12; Jeremiah 1:19; Ezekiel 36:28; Joel 2:13; Matthew 28:20; Luke 1:79; John 1:5; 3:19; 8:12; 8:32-36; 14:17; 15:4-10; Acts 13:39; Romans 6:18-22; 8:1-2; 1 Corinthians 7:22; 2 Corinthians 1:20; 4:6; 5:17; 6:18; 9:8; Ephesians 3:19; 5:8; Galatians 5:1; 6:15; Colossians 2:9; 1 Thessalonians 5:5; Hebrews 13:21; James 1:4; 1 Peter 2:9; 2:16; 1 John 2:2; 2:28; 3:24; 4:10; 4:13-16.

[4]Michael Ende, *The Neverending Story*, trans. Ralph Manheim (New York: Dutton Books for Young Readers, 1997), 321-27.

[5]Ende, *The Neverending Story*, 366.

10. Examining Intimacy in Our Gospel Communities

[1]Meg Jay, *The Defining Decade: Why Your Twenties Matter—And How to Make the Most of Them Now* (New York: Twelve, 2013).

[2]Myles Werntz, *From Isolation to Community: A Renewed Vision for Christian Life Together* (Grand Rapids, MI: Baker Academic, 2022), 38.

[3]Henri J. M. Nouwen, *Lifesigns: Intimacy, Fecundity, and Ecstasy in Christian Perspective* (New York: Image, 1989), 28.

[4]Werntz, *From Isolation to Community*, 38.

[5]Thomas Merton, *No Man Is an Island* (San Diego: HarperOne, 2002), 24.

[6]Matt O'Reilly, "What Makes Sex Beautiful? Marriage, Aesthetics, and the Image of God in Genesis 1-2 and Revelation 21-22," in *Beauty, Order, and Mystery: A Christian Vision of Human Sexuality,* ed. Gerald L. Hiestand and Todd Wilson (Downers Grove, IL: InterVarsity Press, 2017), 208.

[7]Wendell Berry, *Sex, Economy, Freedom & Community: Eight Essays* (New York: Pantheon, 1993), 137-38.

[8]William Ernest Henley, "Invictus," text, Poets.Org, accessed September 9, 2024, https://poets.org/poem/invictus.

[9]Family Systems Theory was created by Dr. Murray Bowen and is based on eight key concepts. The theory and its concepts are summarized and expounded at The Bowen Center, www.thebowencenter.org/.

[10]Kiley Hurst, "More Than Half of Americans Live Within an Hour of Extended Family," Pew Research Center, May 18, 2022, https://pewrsr.ch/3yKn2ms.

[11]Wesley Hill, *Spiritual Friendship: Finding Love in the Church as a Celibate Gay Christian* (Grand Rapids, MI: Brazos Press, 2015), 61.

[12]Liz Carmichael, *Friendship: Interpreting Christian Love* (New York: T&T Clark International, 2004), 180.

11. The Art of Friendship and the Family of God

[1]Wesley Hill, *Spiritual Friendship: Finding Love in the Church as a Celibate Gay Christian* (Grand Rapids, MI: Brazos Press, 2015), 55.

[2]Wendell Berry, *Sex, Economy, Freedom & Community: Eight Essays* (New York: Pantheon, 1993), 75.

[3]In the context of God's kingdom, biblical friendship as chosen family is first about God choosing all of us and us receiving the family of God as our new family. It is not us handpicking a family of choice to replace another family so much as it is a gift chosen by God for us that can include or exist in an absence of one's bio-family. The phrase *chosen family* can mean different things to different groups. I wanted to use the term *familyship*, but my students made me promise to never use that phrase in public as I would be considered very uncool.

[4]Joseph H. Hellerman, *When the Church Was a Family: Recapturing Jesus' Vision for Authentic Christian Community* (Nashville: B&H Academic, 2009), 161.

[5]Harrison Scott Key, *How to Stay Married: The Most Insane Love Story Ever Told* (New York: Simon and Schuster, 2023), 299.

[6]C. S. Lewis, *Mere Christianity* (San Francisco: HarperOne, 2015).

[7]David G. Benner, *Sacred Companions: The Gift of Spiritual Friendship & Direction* (Downers Grove, IL: InterVarsity Press, 2004), 72.

[8]Henri J. M. Nouwen, *Lifesigns: Intimacy, Fecundity, and Ecstasy in Christian Perspective* (New York: Image, 1989), 39.

[9]C. S. Lewis, *The Silver Chair* (New York: HarperCollins, 2002), 198.

[10]Nouwen, *Lifesigns*, 42.

[11]Nouwen, *Lifesigns*, 41.

[12]Myles Werntz, *From Isolation to Community: A Renewed Vision for Christian Life Together* (Grand Rapids, MI: Baker Academic, 2022), 94-95.

[13]Curt Thompson, *The Soul of Shame: Retelling the Stories We Believe About Ourselves* (Downers Grove, IL: InterVarsity Press, 2015), 147.

Follow or learn more about Dr. Moniz or her work:
www.erinfmoniz.com, @erinfmoniz on the socials.